EDGAR CAYCE, truly the most miraculous ~~~~~~~
the twentieth century, held abilities well beyond those of
ordinary men. While in a state of self-induced trance, Cayce
could diagnose rare diseases for people who were thousands of miles away. His predictions of both medical and
scientific discoveries have shocked even the most ardent
of skeptics because of their amazing accuracy.

In this volume, Edgar Cayce uses his proven powers to
interpret some of the Old Testament's most dramatic
events and amazing miracles, and to give new insight
into the inspired powers of the Judges and the Kings.

From Joshua to the
Golden Age of Solomon

From Joshua to the
Golden Age of Solomon

(Formerly titled: *Man Crowned King*)

ROBERT W. KRAJENKE

ASSOCIATION FOR
RESEARCH AND
ENLIGHTENMENT

A.R.E. Press • Virginia Beach • Virginia

Cover Design by Richard Boyle

Contents

DEDICATED
TO ALL THOSE
WHO ARE A PART
OF THE STORY

Now therefore write this song for them, and teach it to the Children of Israel; and put it into their mouths; this song will be a witness for me against the Children of Israel.

For I will bring them into the land which I swore to their fathers, a land that flows with milk and honey; and when they have eaten and are full and live in luxury, then they will go astray after other gods and serve them, and provoke me and break my covenant.

And when many evils and troubles have befallen them, this song shall be read before them as a witness; for it shall not be forgotten out of the mouths of their descendants; for I know their inclination and all that they do here this day, before I have brought them into the land which I swore to their fathers. (Deuteronomy 31:19-21)

Self-glory, self-exaltation, self-indulgence becometh those influences that become as abominations to the divinity in each soul; and separate them from a knowledge of Him. For thou art persuaded, for thou knowest from thine experience, nothing may separate the soul of man from its Maker but desires and lusts! (1293-1)

Note

Edgar Cayce ranks as one of history's most unusual men. Although unlettered and unschooled by contemporary standards, the information he has given to the seeking and inquiring minds of this generation is vast, profound, and unparalleled.

His wisdom was derived through his own highly developed psychic sensitivities which enabled him to attune to, and read the "Akashic record." The Akashic record is described in his psychic material as an imperishable record containing everything relating to the earth, the universe, and man since the beginning, imprinted in vibratory patterns upon the radioactive ethers which fill all space.

In the individual, Cayce found a *personal* Akasha, a deeper aspect of the subconscious mind, where the thoughts and deeds of the entity have written the history of all it has experienced since its inception as a soul.

In the mystical and metaphysical literature of the world, references to this timeless and universal record can be found. Indeed, many religious teachings are premised upon its existence. In the Bible it is called "the Book of God's Remembrance."

*From the Birth of Souls
to the Death of Moses*

Synopsis of
From the Birth of Souls to the Death of Moses

The foundation and premise of *From the Birth of Souls to the Death of Moses* is the assumption that Man is essentially a spiritual being. Genesis is the story of his creation as a soul, and then his fall and entanglement in the earth—the fall was occasioned by the misuse of free will, God's gift to his creation, and resulted in the loss of the divine estate. When the sons of God rebelled, they separated themselves from the Spirit of God through the creation and projection of thought-forms. So distorted and adulterated did their understanding become, because of their abuse and misuse of the Creative Energies, that they eventually lost all awareness of who they were, where they had come from, and where they were headed.

But many souls had not lost their understanding. These sons of God were still at harmony with the Light in the Divine Mind (which is the Christ-consciousness) and at-one with God's purposes and love. A spirit of selfishness had led their brothers astray. They realized that only by overcoming selfishness could a soul remain in harmony with God.

The creation of the earth and material form was first only an expression of God, but as it passed through the vast epochs of evolution, the rebellious souls were drawn into it and became a part of materiality. Their consciousness became "earthy" rather than spiritual. They devolved to the extent that they only understood selfish principles and worshipped the force and power of "worldly" things.

Those souls who were in the higher consciousness and closer to the Spirit offered themselves as channels through which God's Love could reach and lift their fallen brothers. They came into the earth to show the worldly-minded things not of this world—the spiritual energies which are found only in the soul, or higher self, of an entity, and have their source in God. Only by seeing the Spirit in action could the Sons of Men begin to grasp what they had lost and forgotten.

When, in the passage of time, the earth reached its fullness, the Adamic race appeared in five places at once, and became the highest order of material creation, yet subject now to all the temptations within that creation.

When Adam fell, the divine drama of salvation began. With the fall of the Adamic race (which occurred over a long period of time) and its waywardness in all five locations, a new plan was instituted—one nation to be kept apart for a special and peculiar service, directed by souls who were devoted to the search for God! As teachers, leaders, and lawgivers, they would direct the evolution of a spiritual consciousness and produce a race of ministers, priests, and prophets to instruct all men in the ways of the Spirit and lead them to the re-discovery of their souls.

The plan advanced consistently with Abraham, Isaac, Jacob, and Joseph. With Moses, it took a great leap forward. When Moses led Israel out of bondage, he gave them an identity and purpose and welded them together with the understanding of "The Lord, thy God, is One." He also furthered their understanding by instructing them that the God of their forefathers, and the God he had found, they also could find if they went within.

There will never be an earthly way to measure how much time passed between the creation and fall of souls to the death of Moses. Was it a million years, a billion, or a trillion? Who can say? At the edge of the Jordan, when Moses died and leadership passed to Joshua, all the preparation and prologue was finished.

Man had reached the stage where the divine drama would be enacted.

Chapter 1

Joshua, the New Leader

For without Moses and his leader Joshua (that was bodily Jesus) there *is* no Christ! *CHRIST* is not a man! *Jesus* was the man; Christ the messenger; Christ in all ages, Jesus in one, Joshua in another, Melchizedek in another; *these* be those that led Judaism! These be they that came as that child of promise as to the children of promise; and the promise is in thee, that ye lead as He has given, "Feed my sheep." (991-1)

History provides only scant information about Joshua. Although he is considered a second Moses, he is mentioned only as "the son of Nun" from the tribe of Ephraim. No other family history is given. As an Ephraimite, Joshua was descended from Joseph, and thus was his own ancestor.

Like Abraham and Jacob, Joshua's name was changed when he entered into service under Moses. He was originally called Hoshea, which means Salvation. (Numbers 13:8, 16)

Joshua was the general who, in Israel's first battle, defeated the Amalekites. (Exodus 17) He was Moses' faithful servant and guardian of the Tabernacle. (Exodus 24:13, 33:11) He was a zealous and faithful defender of Moses' reputation as a prophet. (Numbers 11:28)

He is famous for two miraculous victories, at Jericho

when he crumbled the walls with trumpets and shouting (Joshua 6), and at Gibeon when he commanded the sun and the moon to stand still. (Joshua 10)

Moses acknowledged Joshua as one "filled with the spirit," and in a simple ceremony, laid hands on him and gave him supreme command over Israel. (Deuteronomy 34:9) Joshua's duty was two-fold: to conquer the land and to apportion it to the tribes.

The power of God was with Joshua as it was with Moses. While at floodtide, the waters of the Jordan parted for Joshua, and Israel crossed into Canaan dry-shod, carrying with them twelve stones from the river-bed which, when placed at Gilgal with the Tabernacle and the Ark of the Covenant, became Israel's first memorial and holy place in the promised land.

Later Joshua moved the Tabernacle and the Ark from Gilgal to Shiloh and established his headquarters there.

Joshua put all the laws of Moses into writing, and at the end of his days, gathered the people at Shiloh and drew them into a voluntary, free-willed covenant with God. He died at the age of 110.

This is the outline of Joshua's life presented in the Bible. The few personal features about this man are vivid and consistent. The Edgar Cayce readings add several new details about Joshua which help fill out the picture.

From reading 3188 we learn that Joshua was, like his predecessor Moses, "oft a lonely, lonely man—as man." Although Joshua was the most outstanding of the sons of Nun, reading 1737 tells us many of that house were adept as spiritual counselors.

The Bible gives us only selective details and events which the chroniclers remembered or considered important. Archeologists reconstruct their story from the enduring but mute artifacts they unearth. The Cayce readings bring out the less tangible and subtle aspects of the past, such as describing intra-personal relationships and those perishable and fragile memories which are preserved only by the person who experienced them, as in reading 3509.

From it we learn that Joshua had a nephew who was awed by the stories told about the wilderness and who rendered valuable service to his uncle.

Edgar Cayce's comments to his Bible class complete our picture of Joshua.

"Nothing is indicated about Joshua having any special training, merely that he was a man Moses trusted. He is spoken of as his minister and servant. Whenever Moses received any instruction, Joshua was always at hand—not the 'mouthpiece' as was Aaron, but rather as the hand of Moses. He remained in the tabernacle with Moses for long periods of time. Perhaps Joshua was the channel through which Moses received much of his information.

"When we consider it from this angle, Joshua might be considered one of the strongest characters in the Old Testament.

"Joshua didn't have an educated background. He wasn't as learned as Moses. There must always have been a number of people who were ready to remember that. Consequently, it was necessary for Joshua to be imbued with courage and self-confidence in his ability to succeed.

"We might say he was 'the man of the hour,' the only one who could take over where Moses left off.

"Joshua was perhaps eighty years old when the first mention is made of his being old and stricken. [Ch. 13:1] His life had been rugged, quite different from Moses. Joshua had been a slave in Egypt whereas Moses had been raised as royalty during his early life and didn't have to undergo the same hardships. Consequently, even at the early age of eighty years, Joshua was beginning to appear old. Apparently he was able to rejuvenate himself though, for he lived to be 110."

Edgar Cayce's belief in Joshua's abilities to rejuvenate himself stemmed from personal experience. Throughout his life Edgar Cayce demonstrated amazing recuperative powers. A dramatic illustration of his ability is described by Hugh Lynn Cayce in *Venture Inward.* On the verge of pneumonia, Edgar Cayce willed himself back to health in the space of a few minutes. His own life reading indicated he had doubled his life-span in prehistoric Egypt through self-rejuvenation.

Joshua and the Holy War

These in the earth activity were much alike [Joshua and Jesus] not as combative, as in the warrings, but in spirit and in purpose, in ideals, these were one . . . Thus may ye use the Son of Man, Jesus, the Master, as the ideal in the present and find a new meaning—if there is the studying and the paralleling of the life of Jesus and Joshua. (3409–1)

In a culture which accepts warfare and combat not as necessary evils, but as a noble profession and an honored vocation, Joshua is an ideal type: the devout warrior, prepared by youthful service to command as a man who earns through his masculine vigor respect and honor in his old age; a man who combines strength with gentleness, ever looking for and obeying God's commands, and with simplicity and innocence wields great power calmly and with unswerving aim directs it to the accomplishment of a high, unselfish purpose.

Yet this ideal picture is questioned sharply today by those who look to Jesus' example of pacifism and brotherly love. It is Joshua's very reputation as a religious warrior that causes him to be questioned. Racial and religious differences have occasioned more wars and bloodshed than any other problem throughout man's history. And to modern thinkers, Joshua seems to be the epitome of the ardent advocate of the holy war. How could the All-Merciful Father of Jesus be the same God who could sanction and bless a war of extermination? It appears to be the lowest form of religion when a leader uses God's name as an excuse to invade a land and wrest it from its native people by destroying men, women, and children. Joshua seems to be the antithesis of Jesus. Yet,

4

as the readings tell us, the same soul, who as Joshua was so zealous and vigorous in conducting this war, later, as Jesus, taught us to love our enemies, to turn the other cheek, and went unresisting to his own crucifixion.

Perhaps no single feature of the Old Testament is more abhorrent to modern man, or presents a greater stumblingblock to understanding, than the incessant and implacable effort by Israel to exterminate its enemies.

Yet in this complex and controversial arena, information in the Edgar Cayce readings and the understanding he expressed in his Bible class offer some valuable illumination and insights which are helpful in grappling with Joshua's holy war and its purpose.

The first premise Edgar Cayce calls us to accept is the Oneness of all force, and that God is an active influence in the lives of individuals. In a lecture to the A.R.E. study groups, he said:

"Do we believe the stories in the Bible that tell us God commanded the children of Israel to destroy this or that people? Isn't it the same today? We have a Christian nation founded upon that very thing. Our forefathers came over here and destroyed a people because something told them they must worship God according to the dictates of their own conscience. What told them? Wasn't it the same spirit force? It is the same spirit force that moves into the earth and acts upon individuals, that same *power* which has given to men their development—whether they crawled up out of the ocean or were made complete in the beginning. It is the same power and force that we worship as the All-Powerful God, that has left for us its evidence in the lives of men and women everywhere."

Joshua and a God of Love

The readings assure us that God never changes. Down through the eons His Spirit is the same, one of peace, love, patience, and mercy. But Man in his separation

5

from God has conceived Him to be many things. The needs and development, the purposes and understanding of an individual, a group, a state, or nation often determine the color and form which God is given.

What *is* thy God? Where is He, what is He . . . How personal is He? Not as Moses painted a God of wrath; not as David painted a God that would fight thine enemies; but as the Christ—[who presented Him as] the Father of love, of mercy, of justice. (262-100)

The idea of a war against nations was first expressed by Moses. A war which was to continue "from generation to generation" was pronounced against the Amalekites. (Exodus 17:14–16) He also commanded the Israelites to "blot out" the Amorites, the Hittites, the Perizzites, the Canaanites, the Hivites, and the Jebusites. (Exodus 23:23; Deuteronomy 7:1, 20:17) Thus Joshua inherited these commands and was under solemn ban to carry them out. Yet the question must be asked, was this really God's Will, or Moses' own concept?

Before Moses there is an absence of exclusiveness in Israel's destiny. The covenant with Noah included "every living creature of all flesh." (Genesis 9:15) God's first promise to Abraham was that through him "all the families of the earth shall bless themselves." (Genesis 12:3) The promise is repeated to Jacob almost word for word: ". . . by you and your descendants shall all the families of the earth bless themselves." (Genesis 28:4) Nor did Jacob consider violence particularly meritorious. He was appalled by the vengeance of Simon and Levi (Genesis 34), and on his deathbed prayed, "Simon and Levi are brothers; weapons of violence are their swords. O my soul, come not into their council; O my spirit, be not joined to their company; for in their anger they slay men . . ." (Genesis 49:5–6)

The law of Moses contains many peaceful, universal, and democratic patterns. "An eye for an eye" was not a code of revenge, but a law by which the poor and powerless could get justice from the rich and mighty.

The readings indicate when Moses began his mission he was only partially awake, or aware, and that he chose an error, or "sin" in establishing the righteousness of his people. (262–126) This created misunderstanding, the reading states, and required a full period of earthly experience to undo. (True righteousness is exemplified by the publican in Jesus' parable in Luke 18:10–14, according to reading 262–125.)

The spirit of nationalism which Moses engendered in his people drew out their vigor and heroism, but also created a strain of sectarianism, intolerance, and narrow-mindedness which eventually had to be overcome. These attitudes went full cycle at the time of Jesus and reached their tragic conclusion with the complete destruction of Jerusalem in 70 A.D.

The angry God which Moses gave Israel, superior in battle, jealous, possessive, and vindictive, yet abounding in mercy to those He favored, was perhaps the only God Israel needed and could understand. This God ensured fear, confidence, and loyalty in a faltering people who might not have been inspired by a God of universal purposes and peace.

Moses took a people who had been slaves for four hundred years into the Wilderness. If for no other reason than for survival, a nationalistic and martial spirit had to be raised. Although it was nationalistic and self-centered, the idea that Israel was the most righteous race chosen by a superior War-God enabled the Israelites to marshal their energies and secure their place in a hostile world. The genius of Moses was to give his people a concept of God which spoke to their particular needs and condition.

Israel eventually outgrew this consciousness. Even through the time of David, the Israelites prayed to a God of War. Only after the decline of the kingdom after Solomon and the rise of the prophets did Israel look for a God who could save and restore rather than conquer.

And, as the readings have indicated, the Bible is the complete story, or pattern, of man in the earth. And throughout most of his history, Man has remained self-centered, egocentric, nationalistic, argumentative, vindictive, and warlike. Thus it was necessary for Israel to pass through all these experiences, nurturing the spirit of Truth, until this pattern was eventually overcome.

Through it all, no matter how man conceived Him to be, God never changed. His Spirit remained the same, one of peace, love, mercy, and justice for all, willing that no soul perish.

Joshua and the Heathens

The study of the Gentiles, or heathens, draws several strands together which thread themselves through Cayce's philosophy and enable us to see the war against them in the light of God's Love.

When the Bible class studied the genealogy of the Gentile nations (Genesis 10), Edgar Cayce stated a premise which was followed throughout the rest of their study:

"The Sons of Japeth and Ham were called the Gentiles. Although they were akin to those who became the Jewish race, their beliefs, positions, and places of activity were quite different. The genealogy is given (Genesis 10) so that we might have the background of the various groups that are mentioned later. It is a most interesting study to follow each line as it is recorded, and see what happens to each.

"We see certain ones were supposed to be destroyed, others were not to be destroyed at first but eventually, after they were given an opportunity to learn a lesson from the experiences through which they were to pass. They were to view the activities of the children of Israel and recognize, of themselves, that their own brothers or kinsmen (the descendants of Abraham) had chosen another way of living. They were to draw comparisons between the standards of each and the results of living up to those standards.

"Some were sun worshippers, some moon worshippers, others animal worshippers, etc."

Edgar Cayce saw a metaphysical meaning in the history of these tribes. Each name carried a meaning, he said, and if a history of that tribe (or name) were followed from its beginning to its end a message would emerge with definite significance for our lives today.

A case in point can be drawn from the Amalekites. According to the Arabians, Amalek was descended from Ham, the son whose seed was cursed by Noah. Yet most traditions agree that Amalek was the grandson of Esau, that son of Isaac who sold his birthright for pottage.

Amalek translates as "valley dweller" or "he that licks up (or consumes)." The Amalekites are a kind of archenemy of Israel. Whenever they are mentioned in the Bible it is in connection with raids, bloodshed, and violence. They were the first nation to make war on Israel. This battle occurred immediately after the Exodus at Rephidim, when Israel was at its weakest. The object of this raid, one authority states, was to capture the well which had miraculously appeared for Moses at Horeb, and demonstrates how completely the Amalekites disregarded God's will and purposes.

According to the Unity Metaphysical Dictionary, the valley symbolizes the subconscious mind. As "valley dwellers," Amalek and his descendents signify *lust,* a force which is warlike and destructive in nature and, when established in the animal forces of the subconscious, is the begetter of destructive and rebellious appetites and passions.

Amalek's father was Eliphaz, meaning "God is Strength, God is Fine Gold." Thus, says Unity, desire at its origin is good and of God; but when it is misdirected by the carnal man it becomes lust (Amalek).

Thus it is easy to see why Moses pronounced a perpetual war on Amalek, and why Samuel later commanded King Saul to completely annihilate them. Metaphysically, they are an ever-present threat and enemy to the Spirit within.

Although it is always difficult to tell when a man or prophet is speaking out of his own mind, or when God is speaking through him, Edgar Cayce felt the pronouncements against the Amalekites must have been according to God's will because Israel was later punished for not carrying out this order.

The following represents some of his thinking on the Amalekite question.

"Do you think God today tells anyone to go and kill people? Let's get a practical, personal application of this. We understand that it is God's purpose to make the earth His footstool. Consequently, whatever stands in the way of that purpose must eventually be eradicated. The character of the Amalekites at that time was such that they were unclean beasts before the Lord. This was because of the manner in which they conducted themselves toward their own people as well as their servants by conquest. Thus these people who were living in the promised land were abominations. God's People, those who professed Him above all other gods as the one and only God, could not be trusted with the Amalekites. If they were to be established in the land promised to them, the Amalekites would have to be eliminated. There was too great a risk of contamination if they were permitted to survive. Even under the best conditions, it is a great task to keep a large number of people in line. The presence of the Amalekites threatened everything that had been accomplished thus far.

"The Amalekites seemed always headed in this direction. They were the first to war against Israel after the release from bondage . . . Their utter destruction was prophesied then. The only way this prophecy could not have been fulfilled was if the Amalekites repented and changed their ways. But they did not.

"It has been said that God will not always wink at the wickedness of a nation. There will come a time when it has to pay, just as it will with America . . . No nation 'gets by' with anything any more than an individual does. We have to pay every whit.

"Some individuals, and even nations, may be Amalekites today. That influence, that desire of the Amale-

10

kites rules in certain sections. When we light a match we can see the flame until it burns out. But even when we no longer see the light, the radiation continues. We know the good we do lives on. So does the evil, in so far as it is allowed to be an active influence through our so-called Amalekites."

The Kenite tribe points up another lesson. Whereas many tribes were to be destroyed, this one was spared. The Kenites are thought to have been Midianites who went with Moses and settled in Canaan. They remained friendly with Israel and were protected by them.

According to the Metaphysical Dictionary, Midianites signify thoughts of contention and strife. The Kenites, as a branch of this family, thus stem from the carnal or sense level of man's thinking, yet possess a degree of judgment, discrimination, and activity for good. The Kenites, as a level of consciousness, retain something lacking in the "nations" (or thoughts of man) that must be destroyed.

When Cayce discussed the Kenites, he drew a lesson from their consistency and pacifistic nature. These attributes were godlike and merited salvation.

"Even to the last of Jerusalem, the Kenites were never destroyed. Always they were living among those who were marked for destruction, but they always escaped. The Kenites were nature worshippers. It was from these people that Moses received his education about nature. Moses never forgot the Kenites. Often he reminded Israel about them.

"They never fought with anybody. Individuals, such as the woman who overcame Sisera (Judges 4), performed feats against a common enemy, but the tribe as a whole never took up arms. Whatever they were, they were pacifists. They lived among the people, but were not of them. Their great virtue was consistency. They lived what they believed.

"When it was known the Amalekites were to be destroyed, the Kenites departed from them. They were given the opportunity to escape." (2 Samuel 15:16)

The Amalekites and the Kenites represent two types of pagans, and yet in Israel's relationships with both, God's love is manifested, at least according to Edgar Cayce, who looked for and was able to see deeper patterns in this story.

Tribes like the Kenites, who possessed an element of purity in their beliefs, had the basis to recognize the higher element of Spirit manifesting through the Israelites. Those who made use of their opportunity to cooperate, convert, or in some manner change to their way of thinking and living were brought into new spheres of activities.

Several life readings indicate the presence of "heathens" of different tribes who recognized and cooperated with the purposes of the children of Israel. It is interesting to note that the spiritual awakening which resulted from this contact with the Israelites under Joshua led to later incarnations among the Hebrew people.

Reading 5177–1 describes a Canaanite who "followed with the admonitions and the conversations kept between Moses and the Canaanites" and who made "closer relationships with the sons of Ephraim." This Canaanite in her next incarnation was a daughter of the high priest Zerrubabel during the rebuilding of Jerusalem after the Babylon captivity.

Another Canaanite, a seeress, "caused its own people to make agreements with the leader entering into the land." (3645–1) The entity "grew to understand and accept the teaching of Joshua." In her next life, she incarnated as the daughter of King Hezekiah and fled to England during the Assyrian invasion.

There is an interesting reverse pattern in these two readings. Their lives among the Jews was at a time when heathens were invading the land.

Reading 3479–2 describes a Hittite who "became a companion and an associate of those peoples who came into the land." She accepted their truths and tenets and was of the Moabite family from which Ruth descended. Following this experience, she incarnated in Laodicea at the time of Jesus and was active in the establishment of the early church.

Another Hittite (5343) had a period of gaining and losing. She was among the Hittites who made peace and joined with the people of the tribe of Judah. She gained when she applied spiritual law, but lost when she "persuaded those to undertake the material things" of her people. Perhaps "the material things" refers to self-indulgent pagan practices. In her next life, she incarnated as the wife of a French crusader, "dramatized all her hardships," and suffered the karma of the chastity belt.

Joshua and Reincarnation

In the choice then, let it ever be according to that principle set by Joshua, and yet never given full expression to—although being a man chosen of God, spoken to directly in those preparations for activities of men among themselves in the creation of law and order, morals and health, and relationships with others as ever set forth by Joshua—"Others may do as they may, but for me and my house, we will serve the Living God." Not a dead past, but a living God. For as He gave, He is God of the living, not the dead. (3350-1)

There is no greater enemy to spiritual growth than selfishness. Selfishness is the father of all sin. The source of all our energies is from the Spirit, and if our impulses are used only for self-gratification, ultimately a soul will dissipate its energy and lose its divine birthright. The readings indicate the earthplane is the plane of Application, the testing place for the soul's use and understanding of its knowledge of God. Only by application does our understanding become assimilated and integrated into the soul-mind and body. If a soul dissipates itself too greatly through a long-standing pattern of self-indulgence and gratification over a series of lifetimes, it may eventually lose the ability to manifest in the earth, and thus create a serious obstacle on the long road back to the Father.

All that are in the earth today are thy brothers. Those that have gradually forgotten God entirely have been eliminated, and there has come . . . the period when there will be no part of the globe where man has not had the opportunity to hear, "The Lord He is God." (2780–3)

The disciplines in the law of Moses were aimed at halting self-indulgence. Yet everything Moses forbade was being practiced by the inhabitants of the promised land. (Leviticus 18:27) The prohibitions covered sodomy, incest, homosexuality, and child-sacrifice. The ten commandments were aimed at other temptations: stealing, lying, oppression, dealing falsely, abandonment of the infirm and elderly, injustice to the poor, cannibalism, child prostitution, mediumship, wizardry, and intimidation of strangers.

When Joshua took command over Israel, he inherited a compact, enthusiastic, and disciplined body whose stringent life in the wilderness forced a great degree of asceticism upon them.

Canaan, unlike the Wilderness, was fertile and fruitful, with native religions abounding with fertility rites and other sensual practices. Many of the pagan religions had no other purpose than celebration of the carnal senses. These rites not only posed a threat to Israel's purpose, for the Israelites would easily be tempted by these unfamiliar practices, but they were also a threat to the pagans themselves in the large picture of spiritual growth and evolution. By participating too extensively in a pattern of activity on a lower plane of awareness, a soul can become completely trapped in that state of consciousness and remain indefinitely unaware of any higher consciousness or ideal.

Thus, Death is a necessary experience, resulting from man's separation from God, as this reading tells us.

[As] man's development began through the laws of
the generations in the earth; thus the development,
retardment, or the alterations in those positions in a
material plane. And with error entered that as called
death which is only a transition—or through God's
other door—into that realm where the entity has
builded, in its manifestations as related to the knowledge and activity respecting the law of the universal
influence . . . For in the comprehension of no time,
no space, no beginning, no end, there may be the
glimpse of what simple transition or birth into the
material is; as passing through the other door into
another consciousness. *Death* in the material is passing
through the outer door into a consciousness in the material activities that partakes of what the entity, or soul,
has done with its spiritual truth in its manifestations in
the other sphere. (5749–3)

Many of the pagan lines were remnants of the pre-
Adamic creation which had survived the Flood. Their
physiognomy showed what the soul desired to express
or experience in the beginning. The giants, for instance,
had superhuman physical ability, but lacked spiritual
awareness. They were intent upon increasing their material strength, without thought of its spiritual source. By
projecting into the animal kingdom in the beginning, a
genetic code was created which preserved these forms
in a physical way and were adopted by souls who were
at that level of development.

By eliminating these lines, or races, from the earth,
Joshua was doing a service to these souls that they could
not do for themselves. In their next incarnation, the
giants were forced to take on bodies that were the result of the Adamic creation.

Thus Edgar Cayce's understanding of reincarnation enabled him to see the positive aspects of the pagan casu-
alties in Israel's warfare, such as Amalekites and giants.

"Perhaps by killing these people physically, spiritually Joshua was releasing their souls for greater op-

portunities, which they would not have had in the flesh. Jesus tells us, 'Fear not them which kill the body, but are not able to kill the soul; but rather fear him who is able to destroy both soul and body in hell.' (Matthew 10:28)

"No doubt those individuals were already in hell, not knowing right from wrong, having come down from the mixture of thought-forms with the animal kingdom. To kill their bodies and release their souls was a merciful act."

His discussion of the Amalekites turned to the subject of death, dimensions of consciousness, and salvation.

"When every purpose of an individual is to do evil, then the only opportunity the soul has is to be taken OUT of its condition—which means death. In that case it is not unmerciful.

"Then, who are we to judge? To be absent from the body is to be present with God. From the life and teachings of Jesus, it would seem there is just as much development in other realms of consciousness as there is in the earthplane—possibly more. The test is in our own physical consciousness. If we continually fail to meet the test, He will not always bear with us.

"Death does not necessarily change the purpose of an individual. It merely gives the soul another opportunity.

"If it had been true that wholesale killing of evil individuals could wipe out sin, then the Flood would have overcome sin. God promised He would never cut off all flesh by the waters of a flood. This was not the way. The evil influence cannot be overcome by physical means. It has to be overcome by a change in the heart of man.

"Thus we begin to understand the reason for the coming of God's Son into the earth, to show how man must overcome sin within himself, which was the original cause of physical death; thereby overcoming death itself by his own spiritual—not physical—evolution."

These readings speak of spiritual evolution through the law, or teachings of Joshua.

We would turn again to . . . that declaration [Joshua 24:15] as made by Joshua, which has become a part of the awareness of each and every entity at times during the sojourns in the earth; partaking of the earth, yet becoming less and less earthly-minded. (2072-4)

Let the bases of thy study be the last admonition by Moses, by Joshua, when there were those applications in the spirit of truth, though erring often, of the children of the Law of One. These do, if ye would show self thy abilities to become one with the strengthening force. (3476-1)

Joshua and the Genetic Code

Cayce's dating of the Exodus at 5500 B.C. (see 470-22, A-6) places the life of Joshua several thousand years earlier than is supposed, although many scholars believe the Book of Joshua is composed of legends of a much earlier activity. Cayce's date pushes all these events back into a dim and distant era concurrent with the mythological men and monsters which the readings say roamed the earth.

The age before the Flood was an era of occult projections. The rebellious Sons of God, misusing their creative energies, had used the physical world as the negative polarity for projections of mental and spiritual forces. This brought about the manifestation in the material world of their own spiritual distortions and thought-forms.

The Flood destroyed the majority of these creations and marked the end of this era. Yet many remnant lines, or races survived. (Perhaps the elusive Abominable Snowman and the Sierra giants are survivors.)

To the Adamic race and its leader was given the responsibility of eliminating all the corrupt and distorted thought-forms and mutations which exist in the mental, physical, or spiritual worlds of men.

We Are the Promised Land

The real significance of the war with the pagans can only be made by finding its application to the inner man.

Man values his material accomplishments and those proven principles which bring him success. Thus the divine pattern had to be manifested in the outer world, in the arena of time and space, by proving its ability to conquer enemies, build kingdoms, and ensure immortality and success.

By establishing a pattern of conquest, victory, and superiority in the outer world, man would eventually realize this same force could be applied to the inner self with the same results.

Man's (or an individual's) own inner conflict with the forces of good and evil, of the Spirit with the World, is personified through the history of Israel, with the Spirit triumphant.

In the Revelation of St. John, the symbolism is primarily from the Old Testament, yet everything John experienced was a projection from his inner self, as the following tells us:

For the visions, the experiences, the names, the churches, the places, the dragons, the cities, all are but emblems of those forces that may war within the individual in its journey through the material, or from the entering into the material manifestation to the entering into the glory, or the awakening in the spirit ... (281–16)

Just as the readings indicate that the Garden of Eden and the Temple are symbols of Man's body, the following intimates that the Promised Land is another.

. . . know that in thine own body, thine own mind, there is set the temple of the living God, and that it may function in thy dealings with thy fellow man in such measures that ye become as rivers of light, as fountains of knowledge, as mountains of strength, as the pastures for the hungry, as the rest for the weary, as the strength for the weak. (281-28)

To possess this "promised land" we must become it. And this we can only do by conquest of the enemies within which are worldly and selfish.

Hence, at this particular period when there are changes to be wrought, ye have work to do. For ye have been made conscious of the fact that all have fallen short of their duty, and that if they would bring the earth to be a place in which even their own off-spring would live, they must learn to search for their God. And they must put away those gods of the Sidonians, those gods of the heathen, gods of self, gods of gratifying of flesh; and crucifying the flesh—in mind, in body, in spirit—show thyself worthy of being given the opportunity to express thyself to others. (3645-1)

The body is the Temple—and we are the Promised Land! Only by putting all other "gods" aside can we complete the pattern.

Then, in the study of self, there is the recognition that there are forces outside of self, there are forces and influences within self. The true-God forces meet within, not without self. For when there are altars builded outside, which individuals approach for the interpretation of law, whether it be physical, mental, or spiritual, these are temptations. It is concerning such that the warnings were given to the peoples. Though the entity or others may say, "Oh that's the old Jewish conception of it," but be ye Jew, Gentile,

Greek, Parthenian, or what, the law is One—as God is one. And the first command is, "Thou shalt have no other gods before me." (3548-1)

The Entry into Canaan

Armed now with new insights and understanding derived from the Cayce philosophy, we return back to the Jordan and the story of the crossing.

Tradition states that only two men over the age of twenty-one who left Egypt entered the promised land. They were Caleb and Joshua, the two spies who gave the favorable report.

The life readings give no indication which disproves this tradition. In the following, though, we find a woman whose experience spanned the Exodus cycle.

In both the past and the present, her name had been Hannah.

... we find [the entity] during that period known as the return of the peoples to the promised land from that land of bondage as the peoples were led from the pilgrimage into the promised land. As has been recorded, *few* that were of the age of accountability entered in the promised land. The entity *then, again* in the name Hannah, left Egypt and entered in the promised land; in the household of those that settled in their division of the land about Bethel. In this experience the entity gained, for though the hardships of bondage—as well as those of the following through the various experiences in the journeys—the entity held to that ideal, that that had *builded* the promise, in this particular people, in this particular period.

In the present, this and other sojourns—or travel— are of special interest to the entity, and while others wonder often at the falling away of the peoples under the various experiences and the various trials that arose, to the entity these are easily—or more easily— understood than to many. In this application in the present, the abilities to counsel with, to reason with, the cheeriness of an often counted slight rather makes for a variation in the *experience* of those whom the entity contacts, and a mother to all. (404-1)

Although Hannah crossed over, this woman stayed on the other side. A Hebrew widow was told in her reading she had been a Reubenite, a member of that tribe which chose as its inheritance land that was not part of the promise. (See Numbers 32 and Joshua 1:12–15.)

Before that we find the entity was again among the chosen peoples, as they entered into the promised land.

The entity and its sojourners then remained upon the opposite side of the Jordan, for the entity was among the daughters of Reuben; and the entity then, of course, was among those that were born in the wilderness, yet came under those activities of the teacher, the leader, and the peoples that aided in the services for its own particular group *about* the setting outs for those in the way that made for the *leadings* of those that had their portion of the service in and about the tabernacle.

Then, the entity was of the daughters of Reuben, but among those that were aiding in the establishing of those influences that became a portion of that service.

Hence the entity was joined unto one of the sons of Levi, yet remained with her own people in the period when there was the preserving and the establishing of the lands in the promised land; during those periods of Joshua's life.

The name then was Eliesa . . .

Q–1. Can you explain the periods of extreme doubt that come, though innately I must believe?

A–1. . . . It was innately seen in those experiences when among the daughters of Reuben, in those activities when the men of war and the younger men were aiding their brethren in the establishing of the activities of the chosen people. Fears and doubts then arose. These have been a portion of the entity's experience through its sojourn. Yet, as in those experiences, as were the messages to the leaders from Joshua, "Let others do as they may, but for me and my house, we will serve a *living* God." . . .

Is it then any wonder that doubt and fear still at times remain a portion of the entity innately, and a portion of that development sought?

Yet if the body will put into the activity those truths presented even then, there may come more and more the answer of those promises that were given of old, "When ye call, I will HEAR! and that right speedily—if ye be my children, I will be your God." These are promises, as from the beginnings of the experience of man meeting his own self. Yet, as He gave, "Though the heavens and the earth pass away, those promises shall not fail" to maintain and to bring harmony and peace into the experience of those that will draw nigh unto Him. (1144-2)

The Parting of the Jordan

. . . the waters of the Jordan shall be divided, the waters that are flowing down from above shall pile us as though they were in sheepskins, one beside the other. (Joshua 3:13)

Three times in the twentieth century earthquakes have dammed the Jordan. In 1927 and 1924 severe quakes stopped the flow of the river for twenty-four hours by shoring tons of soil from the embankment. In 1806 the lower reaches of the Jordan near Jericho were dry for twenty-one hours due to the debris of an earthquake. The Arabs record a similar incident in A.D. 1267.

Some scholars feel that the Jordan crossing is only a myth or legend inspired by these natural phenomena. Others feel comfortable with it as the logical explanation, while others will settle for nothing less than divine intervention and the cessation of all natural law.

A similar problem exists for the Red Sea crossing, or

"Reed Sea" depending upon the translation. The Suez Canal now covers what is a probable location for the crossing. The existence of fords can actually be traced along this waterway, making it credible that the flight from Egypt could have taken place there.

Near the north end of the Gulf is the site where early Christians assumed the miracle to have happened. Strong northwest winds occasionally drive the waters at this extremity so far that it becomes possible to wade across. In Egypt the prevailing wind is from the west, yet the Bible consistently mentions the east wind, which is typical of Palestine.

Miracles are not devalued because they can be explained by natural phenomena. The miracle is not how it happened, but when! The mystery and wonder is that when the faithful needed a strong wind or an earthquake, it happened. Time and Space become servants of Ideal and Purpose if they are one with the Lord's. The readings assure us it is true that "the stars in their course will fight for thee." (Judges 5:20)

In all the life readings for Exodus cycle, not one reference is made to the Red Sea, whereas at least two mention the miracle of the Jordan. If, as is supposed, Edgar Cayce was reading the subconscious minds of entities and recalling from them those experiences which had made the deepest impression and carried the most influence, it is curious that the Red Sea miracle, considered one of the most significant and dramatic episodes in Jewish history, is never found among these memories.

The Red Sea is discussed in one reading (*Search for God* series) as a metaphysical symbol used by the teachers of Israel.

> . . . *all* must pass under the rod, even as was given by those teachers that as Moses and the children passed through the sea they were baptized in the cloud and in the sea; as an example, as an omen, as a physical activity of a spiritual, a physical separation from that which had been builded in their experience as the sojourn in Egypt. (262–60)

23

Although the reading indicates it was also a literal event in time and space, it is not found among the personal experiences in the life readings, as the Jordan crossing is.

A possible explanation might be that it was not as dramatic as commonly assumed. If it was due to prevailing winds, or exposed fords, perhaps the escape was overshadowed by later events such as the theophany on Mount Sinai, the manna, the years of wandering, and the rebellions, all of which are mentioned in individual readings.

Winds are not as dramatic as earthquakes.

The following reading suggests the dramatic and literal nature of the Jordan crossing, and reveals a dynamic and unusual Israelite of that time.

Before that the entity was among those peoples in their march from bondage to freedom.

And this will ever be a seeking in the experience of the entity—freedom—freedom—from all forms of counsel—freedom from all directions. And those who make demands, will to the entity, in many respects represent tyrants.

Do not let those upon whom the entity depends for advice and counsel for judgments be so reckoned by the entity. Let them ever know, too, the law is perfect—if ye know the law.

The entity in that experience was born in the wilderness and thus among those who journeyed into the promised land seeing, knowing much about those activities, especially when dissensions arose in those periods when Korah was destroyed. The entity knew then much of the activities and preparations when there was the entrance into the promised land, knowing and hearing much pertaining to the crossing of Jordan, also the walls of Jericho. All of these were a part of the entity's physical awareness.

Hence mysterious unseen, unexplained physical conditions are not mysteries to the entity but are a part of the consciousness of those who attain to a certain awareness within themselves.

Hence the entity as has been indicated is not only "sensitive" but intuitive, as to spiritual, as well as the purely emotional feelings of body and mind. Hence this will present to the entity at times problems, as to whether judgments arise purely from the moral and spiritual law or from the purely emotional influences of the body itself. Then in the name Jeheuthel, the entity was an associate of the younger brother of Caleb; becoming one in power for the direction of many when the tabernacle was set up in Shiloh.

The name to the entity means much, if and when analyzed in self. (2905–3)

Twelve Stones

When the feet of the priests bearing the Ark of the Covenant touched the river, the waters began to rise up "in a great heap." (Joshua 3:15–16) The priests stood in the riverbed until all the people passed over. When the crossing was complete, Joshua bid twelve men, one from each tribe, to pick up a stone and carry it to Gilgal. At Gilgal the stones were placed as a memorial to the miracle of the crossing, the first monument in the Holy Land.

A hint of the significance of these stones is seen by the space devoted to them—a whole chapter in the Book of Joshua. (Chapter 4)

From Josua himself we learn their meaning.

And he said to the children of Israel. When your children shall ask you in time to come, saying, What is the meaning of these stones?

Then you shall explain them to your children, and say to them . . . So that all the peoples of the earth might know that the hand of the Lord is mighty, and that you may worship the Lord your God forever. (Joshua 4:21–24)

One cannot study Cayce's Bible without coming to realize the organic structure and unity of the Book. The Bible is a book of patterns for man's unfoldment which are fulfilled through cycles of experience. The cycles repeat themselves; but as an individual grows in awareness, or "unfolds" he perceives the patterns of life on an ever-broadening field of consciousness.

Although Jacob, when he had his dream, slept on a stone (Genesis 28:18), and set up a pillar of stone (Genesis 35:14), and Moses wrote the law on tablets of stone (Exodus 28:11, 12), it isn't until Joshua that we have twelve stones.

Jesus spoke of himself as the "cornerstone" and quoted Psalm 118: "The stone which the builder rejected has become the head of the corner." But Jesus was not referring to himself as a man, but rather to his spirit, or the consciousness he had obtained. This was the same consciousness which was in Peter, enabling him to see Jesus as the Messiah, or a son of the living God. This was the consciousness Peter was in when Jesus said to him, "You are the stone, and upon this stone I will build my church." (Matthew 16:18)

Q–3. What is the Holy Church?
A–3. That which makes for the awareness in the heart of the individual . . . The Church is never a body, never an assembly. An *individual* soul becomes aware that it has taken that Head, that Son, that Man even, to be the intermediator. *That* is the Church . . . What readest thou? "Upon this I will build my church." What church? . . . here ye may find the answer again to many of those questions concerning the Spirit, the Church, the Holy Force that manifests by the attuning of the individual, though it may be for a moment. He asked, "Whom say men that I am?" Then Peter answered, "Thou art the Christ, the son of the living God!" . . . He said to Peter, "Flesh and blood— *flesh* and blood—hath not revealed this unto thee, but my Father which is in heaven!" Heaven? Where?

Within the hearts, the minds; the place where Truth is made manifest! Wherever Truth is made manifest it gives place to that which is heaven *for those that seek* and love truth! (262-87)

In verse 5, Joshua tells the men to "take up every man of you a stone upon his shoulder." It is significant that this same soul who tells his men to take up a stone, or burden on their shoulders, and cross into the promised land, later tells his followers to pick up their cross and follow him into the Kingdom of Heaven. The pattern stays the same, just occurring at different levels of awareness and indicating the level of development which has been attained.

One of the central symbols in the Old Testament is the Temple built by Solomon. Twelve is a number representing wholeness, completeness, and is thus a foundation number.

The twelve stones which Joshua carried in were set in Gilgal and became the first memorial, or holy place, established by the children of Israel in the promised land. Symbolically, this might be said to be a "seed" action. Joshua was laying the foundation for Solomon's Temple. As the rest of the Bible unfolds it centers around the building and rebuilding of the Temple, with the final understanding that the body is the Temple.

The readings also indicated the functions of the physical body could be divided into twelve activities, each of which could be related metaphysically to the name and nature of one of the twelve tribes.

Each of the twelve stones represented a tribe of Israel, and the name of each tribe carries its own vibration and signficance.

. . . there is that as may be said to be the literal and the spiritual and the metaphysical interpretation of almost all portions of the Scripture . . . In the interpretation of the Name, then: Each entity, each soul, is known—in all the experiences through its activities

27

—as a name to designate it from another. It is not only then a material convenience, but it implies . . . a definite period in the evolution of the experience of the entity in the material plane . . . For what meaneth a name . . . All of these have not only the attunement of a vibration, but of color, harmony; and all those relative relationships as one to another. (281–31)

Although there are many parts and divisions within man, the purpose of life is to become One, and to be one with God.

. . . remember, it has been given that the purpose of the heart is to know YOURSELF to BE yourself and yet one with God even as Jesus, even as is represented in God the Father, Christ the Son, and the Holy Spirit; each knowing themselves to be themselves yet ONE! (281–37)

Thus the twelve tribes, whether literally as parts of a nation, or symbolically as functions of the physical body, or metaphysically as experiences or levels of activity or consciousness, must all become as one in order to fulfill the holy pattern.

Q–11. Please explain the twelve names which represent the twelve tribes of the children of Israel.
A–11. The same as [the twelve ways, the twelve openings, the twelve experiences of the physical to all . . . the twelve purposes as represented by the activities of the openings to the bodily forces for their activities . . .] the twelve understandings; or the approach to ISRAEL, the seeker—all seeking not then as the expression of self but as *one* in the Holy One! (281–37)

Although we might say that twelve stones find their fulfillment in the Temple, and then in the understanding that the body is the Temple (of which the awareness of the Christ, or God's Love, is the cornerstone) there is one last stone to consider, and this is the white stone that appears in the final book of the Bible.

> *To him who overcomes . . . I will give him a white stone, and on the stone a new name written, which no man knows except he who receives it. (Revelation 2:17)*

Just as the Christ is the cornerstone, the white stone appears to be the capstone in the process of building and transformation of the self as seekers of God, or Israel!

Then in the end, or in those periods as indicated, it is when each entity, each soul has so manifested, so acted in its relationships as to become then as the new name; white, clear, known only to him that hath overcome. Overcome what? The world, even as He ... Then the interpretation is that they *have* overcome, they *have* the new name, they *have* the manna, they *have* the understanding, they *have* their relationships as secure in the blood of the Lamb! (281-31)

The Book of Joshua and the action of entering the promised land are extremely important in many respects. Not only did the series of miraculous and dramatic events of the Entry set the tone for the next phase of Israel's unfoldment, but Joshua laid the foundation for a symbol which can only find its fulfillment in man.

Peter, who achieved this understanding, urged all Seekers to the discovery.

> *If you have tasted and found out that the Lord is good. The one to whom you are coming is the living stone, whom men have rejected, and yet he is chosen and precious with God; You also, as living stones, build up yourselves and become spiritual temples and holy priests to offer up spiritual sacrifices acceptable to God through Jesus Christ.*

For as it is said in scriptures, Behold, I lay in Zion, a chief cornerstone, approved, precious; and he who believes on him shall not be ashamed. (1 Peter 2:3–6)

Baptism

The readings tell us that often bodies of water provide a natural creative stimulus for many individuals, and that places of activity in past lives can stimulate memories and emotions if an individual should return to them.

We find this suggestion given to one individual:

These [creative urges], then, will find their greater expression near bodies of water, and near those environs where the entity's activities in the earth's plane have been a portion of the entity's experience. (649–1)

Perhaps the same spot where Joshua commanded the priests to "stand still" in the Jordan while the children of Israel passed over (Joshua 3:8) was the place where he, as Jesus, "stood still" when John baptized him. If it was, then the vibrations Joshua had put there and the subconscious associations Jesus had with it aided in the attunement which brought the vision of the dove and the voice saying, "This is my son with whom I am well pleased." (Matthew 3:16; Mark 1:9–11; Luke 3:21–22) Certainly the spoken message could be applied to the two lives!

It was the same experience on a new level of meaning.

Circumcision of the Nation

The rite of circumcision had not been observed throughout all the years in the wilderness, yet it was the first ordinance which Joshua observed.

This was a bold and dramatic action. With one command, Joshua put all his people in the same vulnerable position as Hamor and Shechem had been. (Genesis 34)

Edgar Cayce commented on the significance of this act.

"There is no reference to the Lord calling Joshua's attention to the law of circumcision, but it was the first thing he did in the promised land. He put himself, his army—the whole nation—in a position where a mere handful could have defeated the whole purpose. Joshua was doing what he knew was God's will, and the people were not molested.

"According to the best of his understanding, Joshua was attempting to put himself in the right light with the people, Jehovah, and his own conscience.

"Of course, the weakness of man is the strength of the Almighty. The very fact Joshua risked such a thing among thousands and thousands of people proved he recognized God would take care of the situation."

The Cessation of Manna

And the manna ceased on the morrow after they had eaten the grain of the land; neither had the children of Israel manna anymore; but they did eat of the produce of the land of Canaan that year. (Joshua 5:12)

"Hidden manna" is a metaphysical symbol for mental and spiritual energies which nourish the Seeker after God. To this manna there is no end. It is part of our "daily bread." (Matthew 6:11; Luke 11:3) The manna which fed Israel is also "a representation of the universality as well as the stability of purposes in the Creative Forces as manifested to a group or a nation of peoples." (281-31)

There was also a physical manna, and was the central part of the Israelites' diet for forty years. The day they entered Canaan, this manna ceased and the children of Israel began to eat of the game and produce of the promised land.

There is an aspect of this which is easily overlooked.

31

With the change in diet, dental care became a problem. A need for dentists arose—and this entity was the first!

Before that—the greater period of activity of the entity in the earth—the entity was among the sons of Eleazer and of the priesthood; among those born in the wilderness and one taken when journeying over Jordan. Of this the entity will never lose hold entirely, in its experiences in the earth.

The entity was active when setting up the settlings of the land, in the care for the mouths of individuals who for forty years had tasted little other than manna or the flesh of quail. But with the variations in the diets, this became a study of the entity. And it may be said that among the children of Israel the entity was the first dentist, as would be called today, or one caring for the welfare of the peoples when they settled around Shiloh.

Hence, as we find, an interest in diets, an interest in the spiritual things . . .

The entity in that period was also interested in the character of water, the elements constituting same, those things soluble in water and those acting as an irritant or restrainer, or those causing through radiation those conditions in soft tissue of mouth, gums, throat, or digestive tract.

Then in the name Ersebus, the entity excelled; not only in the administrations to the people in his abilities to care for his own group, but as a teacher, as an instructor. (3211-2)

Jericho

Modern archeological excavations indicate Jericho could be the oldest city in the world, originating in the nomadic world 9,000 years ago. Archeologists suggest that, as early as 6000 B.C., the residents of the Jericho area banded together to form what could be termed a civilized community.

Cayce's date of the Exodus, 5500 B.C., and modern science's date of Jericho tend to support each other.

Edgar Cayce lectured his students on the following topics about Joshua and the Jericho campaign.

"The name of the king of Jericho is not mentioned. Kings then were only great tribal leaders who owned people in a particular area. Jericho was one of the strongest places in Palestine, one of the few which had great walls built around it. From the standpoint of material strength and defense methods, Jericho could have defended itself for years. The people could raise within their own walls all the food they needed, and had enough materials to live indefinitely without seeking outside help.

"Why do you think the spies sent by Joshua went first to Rahab's house? This is a beautiful illustration of human nature. Rahab was a harlot, and anyone who wanted to find out things of a spying nature, would go to such a place first. It is the same today.

"Rahab later became the mother of Boaz, who married Ruth. Thus she is the great-grandmother of David, and part of the line through which the Savior came."

According to rabbinical traditions, Joshua married Rahab and fathered many daughters but no sons. According to the rabbis, Rahab later incarnated as Hannah, mother of Samuel.

On the plain of Jericho, Joshua had a startling psychic experience. (Joshua 5:13–15) Edgar Cayce described it and its significance.

"No doubt Joshua had gone alone to Jericho, to observe the surroundings. This doesn't mean he didn't accept the spies' report, or that he distrusted them, but he wanted to know for himself.

"When the vision appeared, he didn't attempt to run away. Immediately he wanted to know whether it was friend or foe.

33

"Joshua must have been seeing his other self, his real inner self. Notice that the man did not take sides with Joshua or with his adversaries. Rather he pointed out that, as captain of the hosts of the Lord, he stood for the RIGHT. We might say this was the personification of Joshua's conscience, which was not warped or swayed in this or that way. First and foremost he had the real purpose to do the will of God.

"What a difference it would make if all wars could be led by leaders like Joshua, who fought for the Right according to God's viewpoint rather than his own. He stood aside and watched himself pass by. Have you ever done that—seen yourself as others see you, or rather, as God sees you?

"This vision was a fulfillment of the promise in Exodus 23:23, 'For mine Angel shall go before thee.' It was Joshua's own guardian angel, his higher self."

Edgar Cayce's familiarity with the divine and its effects upon human consciousness produced new understandings and fresh insights from familiar Bible stories.

Have you ever wondered how the seasoned veterans of many campaigns felt as they began their march around Jericho?

Cayce discussed this with his Bible students:

"Most of the young men had been soldiers with Joshua. They had fought all their battles with him as their leader. What must have been their thoughts now as they prepared to take the strongest city in Palestine by marching around it and blowing horns? After the miraculous Jordan crossing, they must have had absolute confidence in Joshua's leadership. They must all have believed, otherwise they could not have accomplished what they did.

"The people had to remain quiet, not making a sound, until Joshua told them to shout all at once. This caused a great power to be generated. A certain vibration was created. Perhaps in the same manner as when

Jesus' disciples shouted at his triumphal entry into Jerusalem. The Pharisees wanted to rebuke the disciples, but Jesus answered, 'I tell you that, if these should hold their peace, the stones would immediately cry out.' (Luke 19:40)

"If you know the right vibration, you can put out a fire with a fiddle. The same principle is behind the fact that when people march across a bridge they have to break their step, otherwise the bridge would collapse from the vibrations."

Jericho figures largely in the readings that follow.

In an unusual reading for a twelve-year-old boy, only two past lives were given. In the most recent incarnation, the entity had been a friend to several apostles, and from his notes came many portions of the New Testament gospels.

In his other life, he was a leader in the march around Jericho.

Before that the entity was in the promised land when there were those gatherings of the peoples from the Holy Land.

The entity was among those born in the wilderness that entered in with Joshua the leader.

The entity then was in the families of Aaron or the tribe of Levi; not a high priest but a lesser priest to whom there was given the mission of sounding the call to worship, and the entity led those groups about Jericho; being among the first to enter that fallen city. This has ever been a favorite story of the entity. Hence these activities—the trumpet has ever been a favorite instrument but the reed will bring to the entity a greater accord or attunement to the needs or the use of same in the meditating periods for the entity—in interpreting the temperaments or moods for the experiences of the entity.

The abilities of the entity are for a leader as to information, from that period. Now it may be put into order as a reporter, a writer of events; and especially sports or those of that nature as would have to do with such activities. These may be a part of the entity's experience.

The name then was Jubeel. (3183-1)

The parents of a three-year-old boy were told their son had marched around Jericho—and also was among the first to enter.

... the entity was in the earth during those periods when there was the choosing of the individuals who were to bear the rams' horns when there was the marching of the children of Israel in the wilderness, after the setting up of the Tabernacle and the ordaining of the priests; when individuals were set to perform certain offices.

The entity was among those who marched around Jericho. This was the high point in the experience or the unfoldment of the entity, as Abajalon; for he was among the first of those to enter the city when the walls came down.

In the experience the entity was a leader, a musician, a director, a historian. For he was also the scribe to Joshua when there was especially the drawing of lots, in those activities that followed Jericho. (2922-1)

This reading describes an experience of one of the enemies—an entity who was *inside* Jericho when the walls came down.

... the entity was in that land when there was the return of the peoples to the promised land from exile, and the entity among those who resisted the return to that land under the leadership of him who crossed into the land. The entity then in the name Rahai, and the entity was among those who defended the walls of Jericho when it came down; and the entity has in the present experience that innate feeling as regarding the children of Promise, see? (2734-1)

When they were ready to circle Jericho for the seventh and last time, Joshua announced to Israel they were to spare Rahab and her family, and were not to confiscate any "devoted things." All the spoil was intended for the treasury of the Lord.

But the children of Israel committed a trespass in the devoted things; for Achan, the son of Carmi, the son of Zabdi, the son of Zerah, of the tribe of Judah, took some of the devoted things, and hid them; and the anger of the Lord was kindled against the children of Israel. (Joshua 7:1)

Following their victory over Jericho, the children of Israel went out to do battle against the men of Ai. As this tribe was small in number, Joshua sent only three thousand men against them—and was defeated!

The cause of the defeat is definitely placed on the weakness of Israel rather than the strength of the enemy.

And the Lord said to Joshua. . .
Israel has sinned, and they have also transgressed the commandment which I commanded them; for they have taken some of the devoted things, and have also stolen, and lied, and they have hidden them among their own stuff. (Joshua 7:10–11)

The transgressor is found to be Achan, the son of Carmi. Not only had he broken God's commandment concerning Jericho, but he had lied and stolen as a result of it. Achan's trespass was a sort of "psychic infection" in the body of Israel. Just as in the physical readings a major illness was often traced to some form of misalignment in the body, so too did Achan's activity throw the whole body of Israel out of its attunement with God.

Edgar Cayce's lesson to the Bible class was as follows:

"According to profane history Achan's wife wanted to 'get into society.' She persuaded him to take the forbidden things. It seems almost unbelievable that one man's sin could effect a whole nation, but the same is true today. The more purified a people become, the more prominent the sinners. One drop of ink will discolor a whole glass of water.

"Joshua realized Achan's sin could destroy the people. The destructive thought which entered had to be nipped in the bud. Achan had to be put to death, as a lesson to all.

"The prince of this world is the devil, and he has his moments with most of us. When those moments overpower us, and are able to influence God's elect, then we will be destroyed—either according to man-made law or our own. Remember Judas. He committed suicide after he understood what he had done.

"When the trouble arose, in order to locate the source of the problem, the people prepared themselves through prayer and meditation. We don't try this very often, but it is a sure way of getting at the seat of any turmoil that may arise. We think we believe this, but we seldom practice it."

In 1943, a young Illinois housewife was told she had been Achan's daughter—and felt the punishment unjust!

Before that we find the entity was in the land when the children of Promise entered into the promised land, when there were those whose companion or whose father sought for the gratifying of selfish desires in gold and garments and in things which would gratify only the eye. The entity was young in years and yet felt, as from those things which were told the entity, that a lack of material consideration was given the parent.

The name then was Suthers. (5366-1)

When Achan's trespass was confirmed by uncovering the hidden spoil in his tent, Joshua ordered him to be stoned, then burned with the loot. (Joshua 7:20–24)

And they raised over him a great heap of stones which remain to this day. So the Lord turned from his fierce anger. Therefore the name of that place is called Valley of Achan, to this day. (Joshua 7:26)

Although by modern standards, this punishment seems excessive, these people were living their faith. Achan's trespass was a violation of a command which had proven itself to be divine among them. This trepass led to unnecessary defeat and slaughter of their own people. Excessive or not by our standards, we see punishment as having a beneficial effect on the moral consciousness of an associate of Achan.

Before that the entity was an associate of Achan (not a companion), that one who partook of the beauty of physical things for selfish purposes.

These brought doubts and fears. These have ever been hard to understand by the entity, the things brought about because of those disturbances giving to the entity an ideal and an idea as to morals, as to associates, as to things not ordinarily found—yet the entity can rarely find words to give expression to same.

Throughout that period the entity gained. Learn to apply those tenets as taught, as may be gained from that experience, in the life today; and being true to thyself ye will not be false to others. And as ye treat thy fellow man ye are treating thy Maker.

The name then was Asbythen. (3578-1)

The purification achieved its desired effect. The children of Israel were once again aligned with Creative Force. In their next encounter with the children of Ai, they were victorious.

In this reading we find an entity with whom we might easily identify. She had been present at the fall of Jericho and those activities around Jericho, which would include the punishment of Achan. She had seen these events, been part of them, yet never understood their significance.

39

How many great spiritual events are occurring around us today that we fail even to see much less to learn from and make application in our own lives?

Before that the entity was in the promised land, in those periods when there was the entering into the Holy Land.

Though the entity was among those born in the wilderness, it was acquainted with and aware of those leaders of that trek from Egypt to the Holy Land, and had a knowledge of the law. Though the entity was close to those who were to administer same, the reckoning which came from those who partook of things when there were the activities around Jericho the entity never, NEVER interpreted in its own experience.

And such routine still becomes at times a drudge. But the very activities of the entity, as an associate of the wife of Eleazer, in the preparation of those oils and the incense for the service, give the entity's present abilities in the preparing of compounds of such natures. These have not in the present been made compatible with the experience there, in those activities about Shiloh, where the entity lived during that latter sojourn.

The name then was Adajoniah. (2900-2)

Treaties with the Pagans:
Joshua Deceived

And when the inhabitants of Gibeon heard what Joshua had done to Jericho and Ai, they worked subtly, and prepared provisions, and laid old sacks upon their asses, and wine skins, old, torn, and patched; They put on old shoes, or bound their feet with sandals, and dressed in old garments; and all the bread of their provisions was dry and mouldy.

And they went to Joshua to the camp at Gilgal, and said to him and to the men of Israel, we have come from a far country; and therefore make a treaty with us. . . . Moreover they also said to Joshua, this bread we took hot out of our ovens on the day we came forth to go to you; but now, behold it is dry and mouldy. And these wineskins were new, and behold, they are worn out; and these our garments and shoes were new, behold they are old because the journey was very long.

And the men took of their provisions and went away, and the Israelites did not ask counsel from the Lord.

And Joshua made peace with them, and he made a treaty with them to let them live; and the princes of the congregation swore to them. (Joshua 9:3–6, 12–15)

This clever ruse by the Gibeonites ensured their survival, although when Joshua discovered the deception he relegated them to a servile position as gatherers of wood and drawers of water for his congregation. (Joshua 9:27) When five pagan kings banded together to retaliate on the Gibeonites, the Gibeonites called upon Joshua to honor the treaty and defend them. This occasioned the miraculous battle when the sun stood still. (Joshua 10:1–14)

The crafty Gibeonites and Joshua's reactions drew out these comments from Edgar Cayce.

"Here we have one instance where Joshua disobeyed the command given by Moses. There is nothing to indicate that he was punished for this, except the fact that having made a promise, his conscience held him to it, even though later it proved to be his people's downfall.

"From the very beginning, God's command had been that all those in the promised land were to be destroyed; the children of Israel were not to make peace with any of them . . .

"Heretofore, whenever a problem of this kind had come up, Moses AND Joshua went to the Lord with it, and asked what to do. This time Joshua failed to do that. So far as we know, he was not rebuked for it, though he realized later he had made a mistake. Several hundred years later those same people with whom Joshua made peace rose up and became the thorn in the flesh of the Israelites.

"Why Joshua wasn't rebuked for this weakness as Moses was, we cannot say. Nothing is said about what he was to lose by it. Having made the league with these people, Joshua remained true to it, even though they had been insincere and used trickery to persuade him. He took them at their word."

Cayce found another lesson in Joshua's reaction.

"Most of the old patriarchs possessed a quality that we do not—patience; at least they manifested it more. When analyzing the spiritual attributes that God first manifested in the world, we come to Time, Space, and Patience. Apparently they are far apart, but those who have learned patience know that there is no time or space.

"We find patience manifested in Abraham, Isaac, and in Jacob, and especially Joshua. We do not find reference to a single instance in which Joshua lost his patience. Perhaps he used bad judgment at times, but he didn't lose patience."

In February, 1944, a thirty-five-year-old school teacher was told he had been a Hittite. The reading indicates he may have had a hand in trying Joshua's patience.

Before that the entity was in the Holy Land when there were those gatherings of the people from other lands. Ye were among the natives, but ye were "smart" as it were, for ye were among those who used Joshua to make peace—for ye were among the Hittites, in the name then Jebel.

It is well to be subtle, but don't fool yourself—and you know you're not fooling yourself, even when you fool others. But ye used this to good account for the material gains. Did ye use it as well for the spiritual gains? "Not by might and power, but by my spirit,

42

sayeth the Lord." This learn in all of thy undertakings.
(3689–1)

The entity remained "smart" and his ability to get
ahead extended into his succeeding lives. In Rome he
gained power by associating with Julius Caesar. Cayce
warned him he would have his own Brutus in the present if he didn't learn to trust his Creator. In his most
recent incarnation, he had been a Forty-niner in California. He was smart enough to find the gold, but lacked
wisdom in how to use it.

Thus there are karmic patterns he must learn to undo
that stem back to his deceptions with Joshua.

Other Convenants

Although Joshua was interdicted by Moses not to spare
any tribe, the readings indicate that, in addition to the
Gibeonites, compacts and agreements were made with
other tribes.

Although many reasons have been given, both literally
and metaphysically, why all the tribes weren't destroyed,
Edgar Cayce advanced a suggestion to the Bible class
which was logical and probable.

"For some reason, many groups were not destroyed.
Later, Joshua condemned himself for allowing this condition to come to pass. Of course, they attempted to
make slaves of the unconquered people, but it was
not always possible to do this. Perhaps these people
were gifted in trades which the Israelites thought
necessary for their own welfare. For instance, the Israelites had no experience mining or refining gold, iron,
metal, or brass. They had worked in Egypt with these
after they had been prepared, but knew nothing about
their preparation. Perhaps this is why certain groups
were spared. The children of Israel were acquiring
knowledge in forbidden ways, and they paid the price
for it. Later, the very groups they preserved were their
own undoing."

In 1940, a young man was told he had been among the Jebusites. Perhaps his abilities as a herdsman and in animal husbandry ensured his survival:

Before that the entity was in the Palestine land, during those periods when there were the hordes or numbers of people entering under the leadership or direction of Joshua.

The entity was among the Jebusite peoples who made agreements with those peoples; hence dwelt among them, because of their POSSESSIONS of the land. Yet because of the agreements or compacts made between the two, the entity was a herdsman—or the keeper for those who had great herds through the land of the valleys, in those portions of that land.

There we find that in the keeping of the entity's activities great help came to many from the material standpoint, and great help came to the entity through the mental and physical relationships with those people, because of their activities in relationships to Creative Forces; and their MORAL actions brought better influences in those groups to which the entity belonged. The name then was Jezeel. (2322-2)

Just as five kings united in war (Joshua 9, 10), apparently other tribes united to make peace.

In reading 2998, a young man was told he had been a leader in this attempt and caused Joshua "to falter."

. . . the entity was in the Holy Land, when those groups of people were entering from the Egyptian land.

The entity then was among those who made overtures for a united effort in making peace with the leader of those groups, and thus—as termed by some —caused even Joshua to falter.

Yet these abilities make in the present for that ability to make peace, and to make for organized effort where the spirit of the law, rather than the letter of the law, may be applied in its relationships and its dealings with others.

The name was Jabeliel. (2998–2)

Division of the Land

Bible scholars and critics generally agree on the historical validity of the person Joshua, but disagree on the extent of his accomplishments. Traditionally, Joshua is considered to have conquered all the promised land except for a narrow strip along the eastern sea coast in one single, concentrated campaign. Few consider this to be historical fact. They also think the allotment and occupation of the conquered districts in orderly sequence also has to be abandoned as unhistorical. These views are based upon archeological evidence and a comparison with the Book of Judges which shows the invasion of Canaan was carried out through a series of successive campaigns over a long period of time, often suffering serious reversals.

The archeological evidence is hard to refute and a historical or literal level would suggest Joshua did not perform in his lifetime all the conquering and unifying that is attributed to him. However, stripping away all the myth and legend, the experts still agree Joshua was a great and gifted leader.

But whatever mark he may have left on the material world, the readings would assure us, is only a dim indication of his real effectiveness and accomplishment on the mental and spiritual planes. This is why all the myth and legends collect around his name.

Things happen first in Spirit before they are sensed by the Mind or seen in the world. The material world is a shadow of spiritual truths. Thus, the readings tell us, whatever the finite mind observes in the material world is already a past condition in the spiritual planes. Man is ever observing in the present what has already taken place. (3744–4 and 900–24) This is an unsettling notion, but one that leads us to see how, in the real sense, Joshua did all that is attributed to him. If the Lamb was slain before the foundation of the world (Revelation 13:8) when the soul of Jesus made his offering in the spiritual world (262–57), then, before Israel ever crossed the Jordan, the promised land had already been conquered and the inheritance apportioned. It was already a past fact in the mind of Joshua. In mind and spirit he had done everything necessary to ensure its appearance in time and space.

God doesn't look on things from the physical standpoint, as we do. Though it may take a long time to appear, He never forgets that there was a time when souls, or a soul, made all the overtures and activities necessary for keeping the faith. For several hundred years after David's death, God said many times, "I will do this for my servant David's sake." This was because that soul, like Joshua, implanted in his relationships with his fellow men something that was representative of God's influence in the earth.

The following readings show several entities who were involved with the dividing of the new land and establishing its boundaries.

Mr. 4052 was told he had made a strong effort to keep the people in touch with their spiritual leaders.

> . . . the entity was in the Holy Land where the entity was with the mighty groups of people who thronged from the Egyptian land. The entity was among those who were in authority, in the name Othiel and was the child of Dan.
>
> Thus, northernmost portions of the land or boundaries have a particular call to the entity. The entity was among those who kept quite a balance between the united efforts of those peoples when once settled, in keeping in touch with those in spiritual authority at Shiloh. (4052–1)

Mr. 3203 was told he had been an Edomite who assisted the Israelites in marking out and dividing the land.

His activities then carried over as special interests in the present.

Before that the entity was in the Holy Land during those periods when the children of promise entered. The entity was one in authority in the land, being of the children of Esau or Edom. Hence we find those various differences as arose.

But the entity was among those that became aware of the activities that had been indicated through the service rendered a people by the two faithful patriarchs Joshua and Caleb.

Hence the entity joined with those forces, those influences ...

In the experience the entity advanced. For, through those efforts in the latter part of its sojourn, the entity aided in specifying and marking out the land marks for many of those varied groups of the varied tribes, as the land was divided.

Divisions and subdivisions of cities, then, of states, and their boundaries became of special interest to the entity, as these things are applied in the daily life of various groups in various portions of any land. (3203-1)

Mr. 3001 was kin to the discredited rebel Korah, which delayed his acceptance by those who were in authority. This rejection bore bitter fruit. In his next life, the entity had had a compelling desire to make himself known among his brothers. As Benaiah, he rose in authority during the time of Solomon. Due to his lack of consideration and the stress he put upon the people, he added to those influences which caused his people to rebel and gradually lose their understanding of God's ways.

Before that the entity was in the land when there were those journeyings into the Holy Land.

The entity was among those of the tribe of Levi

that were acquainted with, and of the family of, those that rebelled. Though the entity himself was not lost in the destruction of the sons of Korah, the entity became so awed and so evilspoken of in many quarters that it was in the latter portion of the entity's sojourn before he was wholly accepted into the activities that brought the distributing of the gifts of the cities, or of the activities, to the children of Levi.

In the city near Ramah did the entity then dwell, in the name Keldebah. The entity gained much, for it attempted to apply those tenets that had become a part of the activities—in the latter portion of its sojourn.

And those experiences in the present—material gains are little, unless the mental and the spiritual are in accord with same. (3001–1)

Caleb and His Family: The Present

When a Jewish business man requested a reading for his three-year-old son, he had no idea he was adding another chapter to Edgar Cayce's story of the Old Testament.

Cayce, who never recalled a word spoken during a reading, often experienced a recurrent dream of entering a great hall where he was handed the soul's record. During this reading, Cayce dreamed it again, but with an unusual variation. Upon wakening, he said:

"It was the cleanest record I've ever experienced. The book is the cleanest, and yet I had never thought of any of them not being perfectly clean before."

As the reading progressed, it became clear why the records were so clean. The child was described as "an old soul, and an Atlantean," one that could "not only make for a development for self but for the world." A highly developed mental and spiritual nature was one of the outstanding influences in the entity's makeup, the reading continued.

An incarnation was described during the gold rush

era in California in which "the entity gained through the experience and never lost hold upon self in that experience."

In the preceding incarnation at the time of the Roman Empire, the entity governed portions of Greece, Turkey, and the Holy Land, and gained materially and gained mentally.

And in the life before that, the soul made its greatest mark as the hero of Israel, the mighty Caleb—who is consistently described as "filled with the Spirit." (Numbers 14:24, 32:12; Deuteronomy 1:36)

The entity was *one* of the two that were twenty-one when they left Egypt to enter the promised land.

Hence the entity was ever looked to as one to be counseled with, as one to be looked upon as a leader, as a sage in Israel; Caleb, then as the companion of Joshua, with the children of Judah that made for the cleansing of the land for that which became the Holy City; that has meant, did mean so much in the experience of the people as a people and of the world; that has had, does have so great a mental influence upon the world today, as it ever will.

For as then the entity founded same, its purposes, its desires, its activities were in the law of the *living* God, that enjoined all those who would to draw nigh unto Him.

And in Him is the defense for *every* ill, for every disturbance that may arise in the experience of the entity or any individual in a material world.

Too much might not be said respecting the entity's activities during that particular sojourn. Much may be read concerning same; and well, then, that the training of the entity include those admonitions of Moses, the leader of the entity then, and of Joshua, the companion of the entity.

For those laws are ever those things that in the experience of individuals in the material world make for a fortress of *strength,* as they did for the entity in that sojourn. (1292–1)

49

An interesting family situation is developed from the mother's questions.

Q-2. What associations has the entity had in the past with his present mother [1294], and when?
A-2. The mother was then the daughter of Caleb!
Q-3. What should be the proper association in the present?
A-3. Much as then. Not that the mother takes guidance from the child or the developing entity. But the day will arise when this will be as the experience. For the entity is one of a dictatorial nature; not as a dictator but as a counselor.

Hence their attitude should be that of love as shown in not merely affection or sentiment but as purposefulness in holding to the truth of the associations of a soul, of an entity, with the Creative Force—God. (1292–1)

The next question shows the father had been one of the spies who gave out the unfavorable report. Thus there will be a sensitive area in the present father-son relationship.

Q-4. What association in the past with his present father [1291], and how may they mean the most to each other in the present?
A-4. . . . In the land of the returning or journeying from Egypt, the present father was then a companion of the entity—among the spies that spied out the land.

Hence we will find in their associations there will arise periods in the present when the entity will doubt its own parent's direction. Yet if these are kept aright they will be made to be more of a helpful experience to both. (1292–1)

The next answer is interesting and emphatic.

Q-6. What type of nurse would be best for this child?
A-6. One that is patient, long-suffering; but most of

all one that *knows* the LAW! Not of the land, but of God! (1292–1)

Caleb's Daughter

From the above question, 1292's mother learned she had once been her own child's daughter. In her own reading she was told she had been Ach-sah, whose story is found in Joshua 15.

As the conquering, settling, and division of the land continued, the portion which Moses promised to Caleb remained unconquered. In order to encourage his warriors to battle with those remnants of the pre-Adamic creation, the giants of Hebron, Caleb offered the hand of his daughter Ach-sah to the spoiler of Keriath-sepra. (Joshua 15:15–17) Othniel, Caleb's brother, took the city and won a bride.

Before that we find the entity's experience that becomes the greater of its activities . . .

The entity then was the daughter of a leader, Caleb, that brought such a report of the land to all those travelers, those peoples of promise, those chosen that were to give to the world the basic principles for their moral and spiritual life.

Then entity was born in the wilderness, and was given in marriage when there was the conquering and the activity of the father's people in the taking and settling of the lands about the Holy City.

Then in the name Ach-sah, and the companion of the entity in the present was then a son of Benjamin —but not the one to whom the entity was wed. This brought in the experience some doubts, some miscomprehensions. And yet throughout the experience the entity gave to the peoples the ideals of a life of purposefulness, even though the edicts of the fathers overruled the hearts of the women in those periods.

Yet these arise in the experience of the entity at times in the present sojourn—that as the heart longs for, as is seen in the experience—as may be attained even by the seeking, the knocking, the working towards those directions, if used properly may become helpful influences; but if they are used as self-indulgences, they become stumblingblocks to many.

In the experience the entity finds from that sojourn that the laws as pertaining to the relationships of individuals in the marital life, those as pertain to holdings as may be said in the material life, become as much in the manner as the entity entertained during those sojourns. Though it brought the disturbing forces in the present, they may be made to become those influences that may bring peace and harmony. (1294-1)

The reading adds a poignant touch to the story of Caleb and Ach-sah. The man she was not permitted to marry in that life became her husband in the present.

Q-3. When in the past have I been associated with my present husband, and what should we mean to each other's development in the present?
A-3. In these we find two outstanding experiences, and yet both were not consummated in the wedded life.

In the previous, lovers—but never man and wife.

In the wilderness, lovers—but never man and wife.

Hence there should be in this experience rather the *fulfilling*, and the deeper feeling that may be held between each that their love-life, their associated life, should mean more than even to others. Not as lording, but rather as fulfilling a *longing*.

And this has been experienced by each.* (1294-1)

No doubt, as one of the unconvinced spies, her lover was unacceptable to Caleb.

Evidently there was at least one Israelite girl who suffered the same fate as Ach-sah.

*In the case files at Virginia Beach, Gladys Davis has recorded the husband died six months after the reading was given.

Before that the entity was in the Holy Land when there were those periods of journeying into the land and settling there.

The entity then was a real character, as the entity was in that position as the daughter of Caleb who was given to his brother's son for taking what was then Hebron.

The entity then set an example, as did the household of Caleb, as did the household of the husband, among those people through those people following the death of Joshua. And the entity was among the first of those leaders of the groups that kept, as it were, the house in order. (3564–2)

Caleb's Family: The Past

A young female vocalist was told she had also been one of Caleb's daughters.

Before that we find the entity was in the Holy Land when there was the entering into the Holy Land of the children of promise. The entity was among the daughters of one Caleb, one prompted to the activities which brought the entity Caleb with his household into prominence and to the promised land. The entity was then one given to song, and the psalms which later became parts of the activities of the children of promise were portions of the experience of the entity.

Not that it is to be given wholly to psalm singing but these should be the basis of the purposes of the entity in its teachings and its contribution to the home. (5356–1)

This member of Caleb's household also made strong, positive contributions to the welfare of Israel.

Before that the entity was in the Holy Land when the people were gathering from Egypt.

The entity was among those about the Holy City that later became the place of David's activities.

For the entity was in the household of Caleb who

settled in Hebron and the holy areas of that particular land.

There we find that the entity was given to good works towards the preparations for activities of those dedicated to the priesthood.

Thus the entity's activities of being as a teacher, as an instructor, as a healer through nursing, through caring for those in need of close attention, may enable the entity to find the greater outlet for itself; as a nurse, a teaching nurse and instructing nurse in the welfare either of the young or the old—as a companion for shut-ins.

These activities may at times appear to become very tedious, very tiresome, yet the joy ye may bring may build all of that which may produce peace and harmony in the life of the entity.

The name then was Adyar. (5018-1)

A prominent Protestant physician and surgeon was told he had once been the grandson of Caleb.

Before that we find the entity was in the Holy Land. For the entity was among those who were of the peoples of promise born in the wilderness, and thus entered with its families and with the leaders into activity in Jerusalem. For the entity was the grandson of Caleb who was given Hebron as his portion of inheritance for the report given when sent into the Holy Land to spy out same.

The entity then aided in the establishing of those activities that later made for the choice by the son of Jesse as a place where a house of God might be built.

The entity then was an herb physician, in the name Ardyeh. In the experience the entity gained. The entity has gained from same in the present, and yet has learned and may learn the more that the personality and arousing hope in the mental body may contribute the greater to the ability for the entity to gain the confidence of and through same be the greater channel of help to others. (5083-2)

Under the directorship of Joshua, Israel experienced a high point in its history. It was from events in this period that later portions of Scripture were drawn.

A young boy was told he had been a student under Joshua; later, an associate.

Then in the name Jarpar, the entity's activities were in relation to the keeping of records of the various happenings that were to be recorded for the instruction of the people later. These became a part of the activities from which the writers of Judges (and they were many) and portions of Samuel obtained their material—those records that were kept during that period when the activities were set by Joshua in the early settlings and dividing of the land.

As indicated in the writings of the record kept, the entity was accredited with the writings of the peoples of that day. The entity is still a student of certain groups, certain classes, certain characters of writings that indicate happenings in groups of people or nations. (4035–1)

Activities during this time were also source material for the Psalms of David.

. . . the entity was among those who entered into the promised land, and saw those days and periods of the establishing within the land of those that had been promised that activity.

The entity then found joy in the expressions with those that aided in the establishings of those periods when, later, from the very writings of the entity the Psalmist chose much that was set to music.

For the entity was an encouraging one to the leader, Joshua, in the experience; in the name then Shumeman, and was of the daughters then of Judah.

In the experience in the present from that sojourn

there arises that which makes for a harkening within self to that which is of praise to a holy purpose, a holy desire. (1035–1)

And there failed not one of the good things which the Lord had spoken to the house of Israel; all came to pass. (Joshua 21:45)

Joshua inherited a compact and enthusiastic group which had been purified through the trials in the wilderness. The forty years of testing and tribulation were necessary to purge the evil, or negative influences out of the soul of Israel. The ones who died in the wilderness were the rebels. Those who survived kept to God's purposes and will.

Perhaps those souls who were with Moses in Egypt had come in with Adam in the beginning, and in bondage because of karmic patterns built through their fall. Thus the period in the wilderness presented them opportunities to re-establish their relationship with the ideal they held in the beginning.

The wilderness-born "second generation" is characterized by their responsiveness to Joshua, and by their great accomplishments after their entry into Canaan. The gates of reincarnation were closed to souls with a low, or negative, vibration. Except for Achan, the spirit of Satan —which is rebellion, or selfishness—was banished from Israel during Joshua's time. Only those who had "the desire and purpose to glorify the Father" (281–16) were granted the opportunity to establish themselves in the promised land.

The following reading describes an outstanding life which epitomizes the spirit of that wilderness-born "second generation," and provides a synopsis of this most outstanding and influential period.

Before that we find the experience of the great understanding, of the greater influence in the present, and from which there may be builded much of that in the present for not only the enduring influences in the material activities but in the mental as well as the spiritual influences.

When there was the journeying of the children of Israel through the wilderness, the entity then was among the children of Judah, born of its parents in and about that land of Sinai when they journeyed there.

The entity was under those periods of journeying, under those periods of activities when there were the turmoils and strifes that arose, and the activities that brought about the purifying as well as a leaving off of those things that had brought doubt and fear.

For remember, the journeyings at the period were for the purpose that those who had spoken evil of the land to which the promises had been given to the forefathers, for the indwelling there for their preparation for a purpose, might be expended and not able to enter in.

Then when the days arose for the preparations, after the periods of mourning for Moses, with whom the entity was acquainted—and acquainted with much of those activities, the entity—just before the crossing over the Jordan—was wedded by those in authority for such, as the leaders and counselors.

For according to the activities, or owing to the activities of the mate, the days for becoming the wife or consummating the wifehood were postponed. For the mate in that experience was among those who, because of representing its tribe for the carrying forward of the undertakings, occupied their place in the line of march.

Then there was the miracle of the parting of waters, and the wonderments as adjourned with the days for becoming the wifehood, and the undertakings with the march about Jericho; and then the friendships and the undertakings when there was the defeat at Ai.

For the entity was a friend of Joachim, who made those peoples to sin in that experience.

O the lessons that the entity gained there! and the beauties and the teachings! Though it was not privileged as a great teacher, the entity gave much counsel during the rest of its sojourn in that land—through its activities when finally parceled with its family about the places where the Tabernacle was left.

And remember that thy body is indeed a shadow of that Tabernacle! For as it was there He promised to meet thee, so now—as in this present day—thy body is indeed the Temple where He has promised to meet thee!

Then as He has given to those of thy understandings, it is neither in this mountain nor yet in the Temple in Jerusalem but Lo within thine own heart, thine own mind, that He meets thee for that awakening!

And when He becomes thine indeed in truth, ye indeed walk with Him, ye talk with Him. For as He has promised to bring to thy remembrance all things, so—as ye commune with thyself, in seeking to be a channel through which blessings may come to others, without the thought of self—ye may, even as ye did as the daughter of Shulemite, and in the name then Marabaa, give to all ye contact, day by day, HOPE and FAITH and CHEER!

For as He gave, the whole law is to love the Lord thy God with all thy heart and mind and body, and thy neighbor as thyself.

Then as ye practice, then as ye manifest those things that are as the fruits of the spirit, so do ye attune thyself.

For know, as ye learned by the admonitions of Joshua (yea, thy Lord!), it is because of failures that sin lieth at the door.

Search then. For as He has given, "Seek and ye shall find; KNOCK and it shall be opened unto you."

WHO will open? Where will it happen? WITHIN THINE OWN CONSCIENCE! For THERE He has promised to meet thee! (1595-1)

Chapter 2

The Book of Judges

The Book of Judges is presented as a history, in chronological sequence, of events from the time of Joshua's death to the birth of Samuel. Scholars agree that the Book of Judges, as accurate history, has no historical value.

The episodes in Judges, presumably, are major highlights of events occuring over a long period of Israel's history. If Cayce's dating of the Exodus as 5500 B.C. (reading 470–22) is correct, the period of Judges could span over a thousand years.

The book enshrines some of the great heroes of Israel and demonstrates that the fortunes of Israel depended upon their acceptance or rejection of God's purposes. Rebellion against His laws led to oppression by pagan nations. Repentance and acceptance resulted in deliverance.

These brief historical accounts provided Israel assurance of God's presence among them.

> While there is the consideration given to all those influences that are a part of man's experience, as signs, as symbols—and while these do have their place— they are not other than ASSURANCES to the mind of man of God's presence with, and direction of, those choices made by individuals (2803–2)

The Judges of Israel were ministers, preachers, and interpreters of the law, arbitrating in the differences between their own people and their neighbors. Usually they were influential only in a small area. Under times of crisis or when confronting extraordinary events, such as meeting a common foe, the tribes banded together. Then the tribal leaders ruled as a group with great authority over a large section of the land. When conditions changed and things returned to normal, the leaders disbanded and returned to their home areas.

Samson was influential only in a small area, yet because he was such an important and unusual person, a large part of the history is devoted to him. Other judges are mentioned as being rulers over all Israel, yet no other details are given.

The threat to Israel from pagan nations did not always affect the entire land. Often it was just a tribe or two under stress. The significance of a great leader, or judge, derived from his abilities in getting the other tribes, not directly threatened, to rally to the defense of their brothers.

Deborah and Barak

The Song of Deborah, Judges 5, is the most important source of historical detail for this era, and the earliest extant one. Interestingly enough, in the Cayce readings, Deborah and Barak supply the most significant body of information relating to this portion of history.

Deborah was a prophetess and a judge. Not because she was a warrior, but because she could see and interpret visions.

After twenty years of captivity by the Canaanites, held captive by Sisera and his horde of iron chariots, the people once again were ready to fight. But they needed a leader. The people came to Deborah for advice. Through her abilities as a prophetess, Deborah was able to see Barak as the leader. However, Barak would not accept this responsibility until Deborah assured him she would stand by him with guidance from the Divine.

On April 12, 1939, a young Protestant man obtained a life reading. In it he was told:

. . . indeed, there is a path cut out for thee—the gods have directed that ye will have the opportunity to show forth thy worth. (1710-3)

Shortly after this comment, this challenging statement was made:

Hence, the needs for each soul, each entity to have a standard, an ideal by which the patterns of the life, of its associations with its fellow man, may be drawn. *And these are in HIM, as they were through thy ex-experience in those periods when ye fought against Sisera.* [Italics added.] (1710-3)

The reading then described a past life experience as Barak.

. . . we find the entity was active in the Palestine land during those periods when there were the judges that arose in Israel.
There we find the entity was associated with the only one of those judges who was a woman.
Hence women have played and will always play an important part in the experience of the entity's life; and the entity will be directed by many, yet—as in that experience—carrying out those directions through the influences for activities in given directions, FREE from those conditions that would bring questions into the own conscience of self as in relationship to same.
As the entity gained there, we may find the application of self in the present through those fields of service in which the activities of others as related to state and nation may and will become a part of the entity's experience. (1710-3)

In the question and answer portion of the reading, the young man, then twenty-four years old, was advised to wait until he was twenty-eight or twenty-nine to marry. Three years later, a young Protestant woman, who had been recommended by this man, obtained a life reading in which she was told:

. . . the entity was in the promised land, during those eras of the Judges in the land.

The entity then was that prophetess who enabled Barak to bring freedom to those peoples. While the associations and companion were of another group, the entity chose Barak as the leader of God's forces in the delivery of the peoples from Sisera and those hordes that were making those people in that period as slaves.

Read oft the song, then, of Deborah, as thine OWN composition, as thy tribute to man, to his efforts when guided by the divine as indicated there. (2803–2)

Gladys Davis, Edgar Cayce's secretary, noted in this case file that the young woman related that she had often read the Song of Deborah and had received great help from it.

Thus in thy present sojourn, first apply or establish self as to thy ideal—as may be gained from the study of the Song of Deborah, as may be applied in the study of the Master's words to the woman at the well, and of those He gave to His disciples in that walk to the garden—in the 14th to the 17th of John. (2803–2)

The young man and woman were contemplating marriage. Evidently a great soul attraction existed between them, due to this experience as Deborah and Barak.

She asked:

Q–4. What are the past associations with [1710] and how may I help him for the mutual mental and spiritual development of each.
A–4. Establish a home together!

As to the associations (that mean anything), these were in the Palestine experience during the period of the Judges. (2803–2)

Cayce advised marriage within the year. Following his advice (and their own inclinations, to be sure) the young man (now age twenty-eight, the age Cayce indicated would be the best period in his life for marriage) and the young woman were married on January 9, 1943, four months following her first reading.

On April 8, 1943, they secured a joint reading on their lives as Deborah and Barak.

Mrs. Cayce gave the following suggestion to the unconscious Cayce:

You will have before you the entities [1710], born February 26, 1915 . . . and [2803], born January 21, 1919 . . . You will give a biographical sketch of their experience as Deborah and Barak in Palestine, the period of the Judges; giving specific and definite information as to their activities and associations; together with the influences and urges prominent in the present from that sojourn and how they are to be met in the present. You will advise them regarding these activities and the urges and influences pertaining to their mental and spiritual development; answering the questions they submit regarding their experiences and associations. You will go into these thoroughly and give definite information that may be easily understood, paralleling the associations then with the present associates and activities.

Edgar Cayce: Yes, we have the records as indicated through these channels, as well as that which is a part of the record of the judges of Israel.

As indicated there, they each had their definite activities; Deborah as the elder in the experience, and the prophetess—thus raised to a power or authority as a judge in Israel; to whom the people of the various groups, of that particular portion of Israel, went for the settling of their problems pertaining to their relationships one to another.

With the periods in which the peoples of the adjoining countries made war upon Israel, or that part of same, the people then appealed to the entity Deborah—in the capacity as spokesman, for the spiritual and mental welfare of the peoples, to select one or to act herself in the capacity as the leader in the defense of the lands.

Then did the entity Deborah appoint or call Barak to become the leader in the armed forces against the powers of Sisera. These are the outstanding portions as presented in Holy Writ.

As to the activities—these, as may be interpreted from same, were close in their associations, in their respect one for the other as to their abilities in given activities respecting the defense of the principles as well as the lands of the peoples.

Deborah, as given, was much older in years in the experience, and a prophetess—being a mother and the wife of one of the elders in that particular portion of Israel.

Those activities together, then, were as related to the mental, the spiritual, and the material welfare of the peoples as a whole.

As to the activities of Barak in those periods—there was something like some twelve years variation in the ages. Barak was also a family man, of the same tribe—though not of the same household as Deborah. Their activities, then, brought only the respect one for the other in their associations, their dealings and relationships with others.

In paralleling, or in the application of the lessons as may be drawn from those experiences in the material plane—these in the present make for more than the purely material attraction one for the other. For, the mental and the spiritual become not only a part of the heart or soul of each, but of their relationships as dependencies one upon the other, that are to be taken into consideration.

To be sure, there are latent urges in the experience, or in the consciousness of each; yet these—as related to this experience in the present—if they are but stressed in their dealings one with another, in their relationships one to another, in their activities and relationships with others—will ensure their own joy, their own happiness, their own well-being physically and mentally, and will also keep them in that straight and narrow way that is pleasing to the consciousness within that brings the awareness of being at-one with the Creative Forces—in relationship to activities one with another, and with those with whom they may come in contact from time to time.

Then, keep that experience well in mind, as to what each contributed in the experience to the welfare of the other, as to their dealings with and the effort to keep those awarenesses in the experiences of others, as to the promises of the Creative Forces, or God, to those who would seek to serve Him.

Beware that there is not the attempt on the part of either to dictate to the other, but rather in a single-ness of purpose may they, together, make manifest in their own experiences that consciousness that was manifested by those promptings through that experience.

Ready for questions.

Q-1. As given, [1710's] activities in the present may become as a service related to state and nation. What type of activity is indicated?

A-1. Depending upon the application of self. In those directions in which the promptings carry the entity in relationship to same.

Q-2. About when should [1710] expect a change to take place?

A-2. When he prepares for same, and as he prepares for same.

This does not indicate that he is going to be a lord or judge or principal or the like, but the contribution such as was made by Barak—which was not as an authority over anyone, but as a director, as a leader for a PRINCIPLE, a purpose, an ideal—UNDER and THROUGH the direction of a servant of God!

Get the difference in these. This is not applying to materiality, not applying to material things, but to that having to do with the basic principles of why and how men think and act, in their home, in their relationships to their fellow man!

This is spiritual, NOT material.

Q-3. What causes the fears and nightmares [2803] experiences when left alone at night, and how may she overcome this condition?

A-3. This should be considered in the material or the physical approach. But if there is the paralleling of that which prompted the individual entity in that experience to call Barak to lead—out of reason, not in its own family—nor in its own household, nor its own brethren, nor its own husband—it will be seen how that criticism was brought at the time. Parallel same for an experience if there were to be such activities in the present, and we will see there is an innate fear when not in the protection of that choice made, see?

Then, the way and manner to overcome—it is not a physical thing but a psychological. Know in whom you have believed, and that the faith is not in the man alone but in the principle for which he stands—as the love manifested or expressed for an ideal brought forth in the relationships manifested in the present.

And with these understandings, these interpretings —in WHOM is the trust to be made? In [1710], or in God? In thyself and thy relationship to God, or the fear as to what somebody will say?

Q-4. In what relationship, name, and activity was [1710] associated with his sister, [1523], and what are the urges in the present?

A-4. We haven't [1523] in Deborah and Barak! We have had relationships indicated in other experiences in the world—shall we go to those or shall we conclude this?

We are through. (1710-11)

The laws of soul attraction that brought these two souls together also were in effect in their first-born child. Perhaps, as the psalmist, he composed the music for the Song of Deborah.

Before that we find that the entity was in the Holy Land during those periods when there were those judges in the land, and especially in that period when those activities of the present mother brought judgments to the people as the prophetess (Deborah), and when the present father (then Barak) was a friend of the entity. It was in that period when, as a psalmist, the psalm of praise was given for the leader and for the peoples of that day. The entity, then, in the name Pithlar, led in the praises—not only of Barak but all the leaders and those who held close to a worship of the holy influences in man's activities.

In the present the entity will find, then, that groups, crowds, throngs, will be those things which will tend to direct, to aid or deter from the fulfilling ... (5398-1)

Another entity was told, in the era of the judges, she had been Deborah's sister.

Before that we find the entity was in those periods when there were those judges in Israel, when there was one chosen of the entity's own sex who was the interpreter for Barak. The entity was then a sister of the one who aided in keeping the children of Israel in the way of the Lord, and the entity gained from the experiences that which brings within its powers in the present of memory, of vision, of color, as of pictures of places, of scenes of peoples who were of its sister through that experience.

The entity was then in the name Shammar. (5367-1)

The Song of Deborah

This verse in the Song of Deborah refers to an actual spiritual law, applicable in the lives of all:

The stars fought from their courses; they fought from heaven against Sisera by the river Kishon. (Judges 5:20)

... as represented in the leaders of old ... if thou art true to thineself, the stars in their course will fight for thee; but if thou art upon those ways that make for question marks here as to thy veracity, thy sincerity, thy ability, as to thy consideration of each and every one in the proper sphere that touches each proposition coming before self, then—as it were—the moon and sun are set upon thy efforts, and the darkness of trouble and discord arises from those seeds of uncertainty that bring distressing experiences in the activities of all. (257–162)

How accurately does the history of Israel demonstrate this law!

Gideon

The next great deliverer after Deborah and Barak is Gideon. (Judges 6, 7, and 8).

Study as to why Gideon chose God. Analyze as to what temporal things brought into his experience. (4047–2)

Joshua and Moses, and most Biblical characters, carried every problem to the Lord. But very few tested themselves upon receiving an answer as Gideon did. (Judges 6:17) He wanted to make sure he wasn't fooling himself, Cayce told his students.

Gideon had a vision that it would not take a lot of fighting men to overcome the Midianites. Victory with a few men rather than a great horde demonstrated the power of the Lord rather than the might of Israel. The unusual procedure was effective.

After his fabled victory, the men of Israel begged Gideon to rule over them. He refused these monarchical overtures, but requested a donation of gold from each man. Gideon melted the gold and had it cast into an ephod. After Gideon's death, Israel returned to Baal worship and "did not show kindness to the family of Gideon for all the good that he had done to Israel." (Judges 8:35)

Abimilech

Abimilech was a half-breed son of Gideon. This son was the opposite of his humble father. After Gideon's death, Abimilech staged a bloody rebellion and slew Gideon's seventy natural sons. Whereas his father ruled only over four or five tribes, Abimilech tried to establish himself over the whole of Israel. With great cruelty, he put down any opposition to him.

It is quite a surprise to find Abimilech appearing in a life reading given for a middle-aged Ohio minister.

Before that the entity was also in the Holy Land during those periods when there were the judges in Israel. The entity then was among the many sons of a judge in Israel, when there had been those changes that brought disturbing forces to the whole peoples—Abimilech.

The entity acted in the capacity of one setting about to establish its own truths rather than those pertaining to any particular group. This brought disturbing periods to the entity, and was not a gaining in spirituality nor in the mental, even though it was a gain in the material.

These at times appeal strongly to the entity, for there comes occasionally the reverting to those expressions by Gideon as to the manners and means in which the words of truth might come directly from the Maker himself.

These are things to be studied by the entity so as to make application. Whom will ye serve? Self? Or thy fellowman, as ye may know the creative forces the better? (3411-1)

Jephthah's Vow

The story of Jephthah, a mighty man of the Manasseh tribe, follows the bloody history of Abimilech. He is the next great deliverer after Gideon.

Jephthah was sired by a Gileadite and a harlot. Thus

he was a social outcast, and turned to banditry. His outlaw band grew in daring and strength. When the Ammonites gathered to make war on Israel, the elders of
Israel sent for Jephthah. Evidently they felt he could do
more than anyone else, Cayce observed.

Jephthah had a psychic experience, Cayce said. He
was moved by the Spirit, enabling him to achieve a great
victory. His zeal was so great that he made an irrevocable
(for him) vow to God. Perhaps, being an outcast since
birth, he felt a great need to establish himself as a patriot
and hero above all others. Perhaps his life among hardened, lawless people made him ignorant of what God
requires.

> *Then Jephthah came to Mizpeh to his house, and
> behold his daughter came out to meet him with
> timbrels and with dances; and she was his only child;
> besides her he had neither son nor daughter. (Judges
> 11:34)*

Jephthah had made a solemn, but rash vow, to the
God he worshipped, and thus felt unable to retract it.

The consequences of that act, a human sacrifice, still
have a subconscious effect on at least two individuals.

The evidence is found first in a life reading for a one-
year-old baby.

> Before that the entity was in the promised land
> when there was the experience of Jephthah's daughter,
> with the return of the father as the leader of the
> groups that defended the right.
>
> The entity then was a companion of Jephthah's
> daughter. Thus the sorrow that came. Thus the joy
> that came from a rash vow.
>
> Thus, it is necessary that there be consideration
> by those directing, controlling the unfoldment of this
> entity's mind, as to rash promises, rash vows, and the
> stress be put in the sincerity of purpose, truthfulness
> of ideals—that must be founded, for the entity, in the
> promises of the Christ.

The name then was Leieh.

In that experience the entity had sorrow brought by the sacrifice of its best friend. Thus a portion of the life was clouded. Not so in the present, if the purposes and ideals are set correctly for the entity. (3089–1)

The second reading was for a twenty-eight-year-old housewife who, in a previous life, had been a daughter-in-law of Noah:

After that [experience on the ark] the entity appeared in the Holy Land during those periods of the Judges in Israel, and in that period of what is oft spoken of as Jephthah's rash vow.

The entity was a close friend of Jephthah's daughter offered as a human sacifice to that overzealousness of an individual entity, who used his powers for material gains and strength, and yet accorded those judgments of Truth; causing this entity, Judyth, to become disturbed, distraught, and to lose much of that which had been the impelling force.

Hence the making of rash vows brings individual activities that yet disturb the entity, as to why individuals vow this or that and then, because they change, the entity can never exactly connect them with truth or sincerity. These bring disturbances for the entity. Yet the entity itself gained. (3653–1)

Samson

Because his name means "child of the son," Samson is another of Israel's heroes whom many believe to be purely a mythological figure woven from the tapestry of earlier myths. However, one modern writer calls him a peasant hero in an era which roughly resembled the American frontier, a rustic with great strength and little brain, who derived equal pleasure from tricking his adversaries, subduing ferocious beasts, and conquering women.*

*Webb Garrison, *Strange Facts About the Bible.*

71

The 281 series of readings contain lengthy and difficult discourses upon the relationship and effect of spiritual energies to the growth and development of the physical body, especially how the mental and physical activities of the parents affect their offspring during the period of gestation.

In one lesson, Samson and his parents are used as illustrations.

In anatomy books, only the physical body is considered or studied, yet the mental and spiritual aspects have their influence and effect. To illustrate the importance of mental attitude and its effect, the reading turned to Manoah.

When Manoah sought with his whole desire and purpose that there might be the blight taken from his associations among his fellows, he, with his companion, prayed oft; and then the visitation came. (Judges 13) (281-49)

At first Manoah was unable to conceive of being visited by an angel, but when he and his wife became convinced that the apparition was real, then conception followed.

The inrush of energy through the mind and body of the parents from their change of consciousness and faith definitely had its effect upon the offspring.

The prayer of Manoah and his companion was answered by the visitation of a heavenly figure, in the form of a man; which was not conceivable by the husband—yet when satisfied of same, and the wife—Mahoa(?)—conceived, the entity physically—PHYSICALLY—was the greater tower of strength. Yet as indicated that strength lay in the hair of the head of the individual. What GLAND caused that activity of such a physical nature, as to be the determining factor in that development?

As is indicated, the thyroid is within the body so placed as to have that influence. (281-49)

The thyroid is the seat of the Will, according to the reading, that gland through which energies pass into the physical body from centers (or chakras) outside the body which enable the individual to hold on to and carry out decisions, ideals, purposes, etc.

Samson, because of his physical strength and prowess, became enamored of his own body, and thus became negligent in the spiritual and mental aspects of the thyroid (or will).

Here this is illustrated in Samson, a lad who grew to manhood with the unusual strength and power, the ability to cope with exterior forces and influences that were beyond the understanding and comprehension of his associates. Yet his ability to say no to the opposite sex was nil—his ability not to be influenced by the opposite sex was nil—because of the desire for the gratification of those activities which were of a glandular nature within the body. (281–49)

Chapter 3

The Book of Ruth

The Book of Ruth, with its serenity and gentleness, is a pleasant oasis amidst the civil wars, anarchy, and warfare throughout the time of the Judges.

The significance of this book, apart from its refreshing view of domestic life and its testimony to love and faithfulness, is in its relationship to what later became the Royal Family. Ruth became the great-grandmother of David.

Ruth and Naomi in their lifetimes were poor and simple. Ruth's marriage to Boaz elevated their social standing, yet they were never conspicuous until David ascended to the the throne. During his reign, the family folklore, probably an "oft-told tale," was preserved in written form.

The story is simple, told unembellished and innocently.

Elimelech, his wife Naomi, and their two sons move into Moab while a famine is raging in Judah. The two sons marry Moabite women, Ruth and Orpah. However, during their sojourn in Moab, both Elimelech and his two sons die. After ten years Naomi returns to Judah, accompanied by Ruth who has vowed faithfulness to her and to her God. Orpah, the other daughter-in-law, elects to remain in Moab.

Although Naomi is bitter about her misfortunes, upon her return she is blessed. Ruth, while gleaning in the fields of Naomi's kinsman, Boaz, is noticed by this prosperous and influential landowner. He is impressed both by the beauty and devotion of Ruth.

Shortly they are married. Their first child is a son, Obed. Obed begets Jesse. Jesse is the father of David.

Following the Book of Ruth, the Old Testament begins to center chiefly on the family of David. Boaz was part Canaanite (descended from Rahab of Jericho, Joshua 2:1) and Ruth was a Moabite. Outside blood, then, was an integral part of the chosen family of a chosen nation. As David is viewed by Christians as a foreshadowing of the kingship of Christ Jesus, this blood mixture is also seen as representing Christ's authority over all nations.

In many ways the Book of Ruth is a foreglimpse of The Christ as represented in Jesus. The actual genealogy from Boaz and Ruth leads to the physical birth of the man Jesus. Yet what is more important, the Spirit expressed by Ruth and Boaz anticipates the same Spirit so perfectly expressed in Jesus. Perhaps this gentle little story, more so than the martial dramas and tense, emotional episodes of the Book of Judges, bespeaks of the still, small voice within. It carries the same message as "Feed my lambs, feed my sheep."

The following readings, a lovely collection, revolve around the events in the Book of Ruth.

Boaz

On July 16, 1927, a successful, young Norfolk businessman was told he had been Boaz.

In the one before this we find in one that was made known in the lands of the day when the entity rose to position, power, wealth, in the name Boaz, and the entity then brought much good to the peoples of that day, especially in the reclaiming of lands for those oppressed, or for those who had lost same, through the laws of redemption of lands that were taken for debt or for the reason of exile, giving especially to the peoples through that offspring that brought David in the land—and the entity gained through this experience, as there was much to the tenets followed, and expressions of action by the entity through the experience. In the urge as is seen, is that especially toward real estate—for the entity wrote the first advertisement for sale of lands in this age ...

In the abilities then:

We find these are many—for in the field of law the entity would have done well. In the application of that as Boaz the entity may do better. In either the entity will find that first self must be conquered, and that knowledge of self, and the principles of the creative energies of force or power must be directed in that channel that builds for the betterment of others. Bettering not in the way of lasciviousness nor in the desires of flesh. Rather in the building of that that is as character and personality in others, and in applying these the entity will bring—through those channels that guide the forces of the universe—those conditions that bring to the entity the knowledge of the life well spent, in proclaiming the day is at hand for all to acknowledge Him, the Giver of all good and perfect gifts, and in that law as was set by Him, give—give—to others that, that each and every man love God—keep self unspotted from the world. (2694-1)

In January, 1941, a forty-four-year-old Jewish widow was told she had been related to Ruth through her marriage to Boaz. The spirituality of Ruth deeply influenced this woman, who, as a close companion, aided in bringing new interpretations of the old order.

Before that the entity was in the land of promise during those periods of turmoils, when there were the judges in the land; when, because of the famines, the associations had brought about periods of unrest.

But with the return of Naomi and Ruth, and with the wedding of Ruth with one of the entity's own peoples, we find that the entity became a companion-mate to Ruth in her preparation and the bringing about of the new interpretation of the old order in the land.

Hence the entity became in the position not of one holding a grudge, nor yet of one holding to a worshipfulness, but rather one who did worship the purposes, the aims, the sincerity in the character Ruth; and her offspring were cherished, nourished, and taught by the entity.

Thus the school, the home school, the home training, the home activities, the home surroundings were a part of the entity's activities through that sojourn; not exactly as might be termed of State, for it was much more personal than the name would indicate.

The entity's activities were as an interpreter of spiritual law, a trainer in the mental environ, and a creator of material and home environ.

We find that these same characters of activity and characteristics are a part of the entity's better development in the present experience.

The name then was Sen-Doer. (459–12)

The widow then questioned Cayce about a prediction.

Q-6. Some time ago a prophecy was given, that she [459] would be to this day and age what Ruth was to her day and age.
A-6. In the son it's being fulfilled. Will that service as in the proper way, the proper carrying on of the efforts of that one in the way and manner as has been determined in self. Then *fill* that, considering *all* angles of the development of that one upon whom the *mental* will fall . . . Stay steadfast in that as has been given, in making thine *son* one as a messenger to many peoples, even as David did of old.* (459–1)

A Protestant housewife was told she was also related to Ruth through marriage. She had been the sister of

*Her son obtained a reading, see 1856-1. His profession is listed as writer, actor, and teacher. The reading indicates psychic development and a desire to serve.

Orpah, Naomi's daughter-in-law who remained in Moab. This entity followed Ruth and was deeply influenced by her spirituality.

It is interesting to note, in this reading, that Ruth apparently never forgot those who were the less fortunate, as she once had been.

Before that the entity was in the Syrian or Moab land, to which the children of Judah had gone when they sought relief from the famine of the land.

The entity there became acquainted with Naomi and Ruth; being then a sister of Ruth; only learning of the needs and that to which one should attain, to bring hope, help, and happiness which comes from conviction of living freedom of experience for purposeful, helpful activities in those with whom the entity was associated, after there were the associations that brought about the conviction of Ruth.

The entity then became a helper in the household of Ruth and her husband; being, then, as might be said, the upper or first maid to the offspring of the sister; seeing then the fields that were harvested not only for the material sustenance of the family but for those also not so fortunate as to be the owners of the land.

Hence the fruitfulness of brotherly love, kindness, and those things that have been a part of the entity's experience.

Then the entity was known as Opaheln; not closely related, but related to that other sister, or sister-in-law, who rejected those truths of which Ruth was convinced and turned again to the husks of self-gratification.* (2519–8)

---

*The "husks of gratification" so emphatically referred to makes a very interesting tie-in with some rabbinical traditions about Orpah, Ruth's sister-in-law.

She is claimed to be the mother of Goliath. The rabbis say that after making a pretense of accompanying Ruth and Naomi, she returned and led a very profligate life. She bore four giants, including Goliath, all of whom were of uncertain paternity.

Although the whole city rejoiced when Naomi returned to Judah, apparently the relative who had taken over her property did not.

This reading was given in January, 1944, for a middle-aged Methodist career woman:

Before that we find the entity was in that known as the Holy Land when there were those activities in which Ruth and Naomi returned to Naomi's own household. The entity among those, or of that household whose husband refused to release or to give the activities or the home to Naomi. These were periods of disturbance to the body and with the happenings which followed, when Ruth became the companion or wife of Boaz, the entity then was railed on by its neighbors. This made for demands and of belittlings in the experience.

In the name then Shulah. (5098–1)

Two days after the above reading, a teen-aged girl was told she had been a Moabite woman who had befriended Ruth and Naomi, and later became a close friend to Obed, Ruth's son.

The entity was then among those who were of the Moabite land and yet, becoming friends with Naomi and Ruth, came into the group activity in Judah, and thus the entity later was acquainted with the forefathers of Jesse and David. For the entity was indeed a friend to Obed, the son of Ruth, the associate who brought those activities to an understanding individual whom God loved.

So act, then, in thine activities in the present that this may be said of thee—not merely by thine own acclamation but by what others see—that ye contribute to the welfare of keeping God's word before others. (5384–1)

A spiritual development expressed through intuition and dreams was earned by a young Virginia housewife during a past lifetime as a Moabite who became a part of the household of Obed.

Before that the entity was in the Moab land, or that close to the east portion of Jordan, where the activities of Ruth and Naomi became a part of the experiences of the entity, and from which the entity gained much of that which finds expression in the intuitive or dream forces of the entity in the present.

For, as Naomi and Ruth returned to the land of their nativity, so also did this entity—as Samoah; and joined with those who were later raised in power through one of the family, becoming a part of the household of Obed, the son of Ruth. Thus the entity was in close relationship with Ruth; and the entity lost and gained, lost and gained through those varied activities.

Thus, from that sojourn, we will find again in the present the abilities of the entity for writing of verse or song, and the depicting of the activities of individuals in the EXTREMES of their experiences in the material world ...

Q-2. What was the significance of the two series of dreams I had a few years ago, in each of which I apparently lived another life?

A-2. Study that as indicated and we will find that ye saw into those experiences especially with Naomi and Orpah and Ruth, and into those experiences in the hills of Judea.

These are the periods, as indicated, when the entity goes to the extreme. Keep that balance. (2175-1)

Although Moab and Judah were traditional enemies, ceasing in their differences only in times of natural catastrophes and famine, when political and religious differences were forgotten, many Moabites settled in the household of Ruth and Obed, and held positions of great authority and responsibility.

This Virginian, twenty-nine years old, was the overseer for Obed.

Before that the entity was in the promised land, during those periods when there were the activities in which there were the settlings of the people in that land—and the activities in associations with others in the lands adjoining same.

It was during the latter days of the judges in Israel; for the entity then was among the Moabite people—Malchor in name.

Through those associates with Naomi, Ruth, and Orpah, the entity came again into the lands of the children of Judah; and was acquainted with those in the household of Obed, for the entity was then a companion of the present companion.

Thus those various activities as related to crops upon the farms, as the distribution of the products of same, were the experience of the entity through that sojourn in its aids to the householders, or—as would be termed in the present—the greater landowners.

For, the entity then was the overseer for Obed. (2301-1)

One of Ruth's most eloquent expressions occurs when she pledges devotion to Naomi and the God of Israel.

And Ruth said to her, Far be it from me to return from following after you, and to leave you; for where you go, I will go; and where you dwell, I will dwell; your people shall be my people, and your God my God. (Ruth 1:16)

The quote and the spirit it represented were used by Cayce to counsel a woman who was having difficulty with her marriage. This tribute to Ruth and her example is a fitting note for this gentle chapter in Edgar Cayce's story of the Old Testament.

Q-5. In what way can I help David overcome certain difficulties and in what way can I help myself with my difficulties?
A-5. In the way and manner as we have just indi-

cated. By living the life to fill the married purpose in the experience one of the other. It cannot, it must not be a one-sided affair. Have the perfect understanding—what has been given by that as an ideal, who became the mother of the channel through which He came materially? "Thy God will be my God, thy people shall be my people!" (1722-1)

Summary

The following readings draw lessons from Genesis, Exodus, Deuteronomy, and Ruth.

Begin and read in Genesis 1:3, and see that it is to thee *Light*, the light of men, even that one who is the Christ Consciousness. (3660-1)

Take Exodus 19:5. To be sure, it is interpreted by many here that the Creative Forces or God are speaking to a peculiar people. You were one of them. Why not, then, today? Although through the years your name has been changed, the soul is the same. Hence this is, as it were, spoken to thee.

Then take the 30th of Deuteronomy, where there is the admonition as to the source, that it's not from somewhere else, but it is within thine own self. For that influence of the Creative Force is so near, yea closer even than thy own hand!

Then analyze that, reading in connection with same all of the story of Ruth as to her sincerity. And if it needs to be, those companionships may be drawn from thine own activities, and the fear of what may be in the future will fade as the mists before the morning sun.

For in the study of these, not merely read to know them, but get the meaning of universal love, not attempting to make it personal but universal. For God is love and, as ye go about to manifest same in thy conversation, ye may find the true meaning of love.

Study also astrological subjects, not as termed by some, but rather in the light of that which may be gained through a study of His word. For as it was given from the beginning, those planets, the stars, are given for signs, for seasons, for years, that man may indeed (in his contemplation of the universe) find his closer relationships.

For man is made a co-creator with the Godhead. Not that man is good or bad according to the position of the stars, but the position of the stars brings what an individual entity has done about God's plan into the earth activities during those individual periods when man has the opportunity to enter or come into material manifestations.

In the study, forsake not, of course, the true way and light. As is given from the beginning: God said, "Let there be light," and there was light, and that light became, and is the light of the world. For it is true that light, that knowledge, the understanding of that Jesus who became the Christ, is indeed thy elder brother and yet Creator, Maker of the Universe; and thus are ye a part of same and a directing influence.

Then, as ye practice His principles ye become aware of same. And these are first: "Thou shalt love the Lord thy God with all thy heart, thy mind, thy soul, and thy neighbor as thyself." (5124–1)

Chapter 4

Man Crowned King

The Book of Ruth closes one era, the Judges. Samuel opens another—the Monarchy.

The great prophet for whom the Book of Samuel is named dominates this early period. Like Moses, Samuel revolutionized man's awareness of his relationship to God. With Abraham, man's concept of God became a personal thing. Moses enlarged upon this awareness with rules, ritual, and laws regulating man's approach to God, yet keeping the approach personal and individual. Samuel, as organizer of the new kingdom, introduced "a new form, a new character of a determining factor between the peoples and the worship of the living God." (1521-2)

This new factor might loosely be called "politics." The Israelites rejected God, a spiritual principle, and turned to man instead. They put their faith in a material principle. With this change came many problems to tax the soul.

If souls in their separation from God and through their evolution have "demanded" leaders, then those who rule us now come from the natural law of cause and effect. Because of the confusion and chaos from the Fall, souls have sought for and demanded order and stability and invested other souls with power and authority over them in order to insure it. From this early development have come myriad traditions, laws, ethics, philosophies, and religions concerning the extent of man's power and privilege over his fellows.

If "politics" is the intervening factor between us and our worship of God, what is our relationship to our leaders? Are they doing God's Will? What if they are not? And how are we to know? What should we do if they are not? Haven't they come to us because we have, like the early Israelites, "demanded" them, and must accept them even if their views and philosophies contradict our own ideals and beliefs?

As we begin to awaken to God and search for Him while in a material world, earnestly desiring to live according to His law, we find an almost paradoxical teaching voiced at times in the readings. We are told unless we can live according to man's laws, we will never be able to live with God's laws. Yet the readings also impress upon us that conscience is the supreme factor and that the Spirit itself is above all law.

The laws of the land are between us and the laws of God. We have demanded and put "Caesar" between us and God. These are "intervening factors" between man and his worship of God. Above all the soul desires to be one with the Father, and only the divine spark illuminating personal conscience can lead an individual to make choices in accord with the desire of the soul.

Souls in their separation created "Caesar" and therefore must render unto Caesar. But how much is Caesar's and how much belongs to God? And how are we to discern and divide?

These are questions which did not exist until Israel institutionalized its government. Under the judges, Israel was ruled only by leaders who were directly inspired by God for an immediate situation. Their authority ended when either the spirit left them, or the task for which they had been raised was fulfilled.

However by institutionalizing power, political factors emerged and are still with us today.

The Cayce readings tell us the Bible is the story of man, representing the pattern of his development in the earth from the beginning to end. Thus Israel's change from a theocracy under the judges to a monarchy under Saul and David is fraught with significance. It is a crucial phase in the unfoldment, yet also part of a recurring pattern.

The original attempt to bring souls back into the Light was by crystallizing their thought-form projections into God's manner of expressing Spirit. This was carried out through the Adamic race which manifested in the earth in five places at once. But the attempt failed. In time the whole thought of man was to do evil, or to put his own self-interests and gratifications above God's Will.

Thus a new plan became necessary: to raise up a peculiar people who were set aside for a purpose; an individual line to carry out God's purposes and establish His Name in the earth; a Name, as the readings state, by which *all* men might be saved.

The new plan began with Noah, who was "perfect in his generations," and established through Abraham.

Thus it became imperative from the beginning that the descendants of Abraham look for and depend upon guidance and strength from the One Source, God, and manifest His Spirit in the earth.

From the days of Noah to the days of Samuel, Israel governed itself as a theocracy. The theocracy of the Judges was a perfect system for spiritual growth. Like a democracy, it afforded equal opportunity to all for expression and responsibility. Anyone could be used by the Spirit if he lived in accord with the spiritual principles which had come to Israel as a heritage and a birthright. Under the theocracy, in times of great crisis or need, certain individuals, often unknown "least members of the smallest tribe," came to the fore and were accepted and recognized as being divinely inspired. Whether shepherd, priest, prophet, or outlaw, they were able to rally the tribes and organize them for a common purpose.

However demanding this method was, it had proven itself time and time again since the days of Noah. As long as Israel looked to its Source and had confidence in its directions, the great men were divinely inspired, and thus material examples of the Spirit in action, working through men.

It could be said, because the Edgar Cayce readings encourage all to depend upon God, that he was counseling in the ways of a Theocracy.

Like all the other nations (1 Samuel 8:20)

The Throne is one of mankind's oldest and most universal symbols. It is a symbol of stability and order, one of man's most profound and basic needs. Thus the Throne begins to dominate this period of Israel's unfoldment, and reflects their concern and desire.

One of the inescapable truths with which the Edgar Cayce readings confront us is that the source of all our problems is from within rather than without.

The Israelites were no doubt dismayed by their shifting fortunes. Joshua was the first and last judge to unify Israel and give them a strong central government. He made them "master of all they surveyed," and the memory must have haunted them. Since his day, Israel remained a loose confederation of strongly independent tribes who, at times, had nothing more in common than a belief in God.

Plagued by bitter internecine war and the threat of slavery to pagan nations, the Israelites wanted stability.

But the fault was not in their theocracy, which had preserved them through the centuries while other nations more rich and powerful rose and fell, but in the people themselves and with their own failure to live in harmony with God's laws.

Perhaps the Israelites were tired of being a "peculiar people" who relied upon Unseen Forces. Maybe they felt the need to get better organized in order to carry out God's Promises. And maybe they were just getting greedy and restless.

When the Israelites became adamant in their demand for a king, Samuel warned the people that their desires were sinful and prophesied the painful consequences of their petition.

But Israel cried out, "No, we will have a king over us, that we may be like all the other nations."

Samuel at first thought the people were finding fault with him, but when he inquired of the Lord, God said, "Harken to their voices for they have not rejected you, they have rejected me."

The choice before Israel was whether to put their trust in material things or in spiritual forces.

In *Politics of Hope*, political scientist Linda Quest gives a lucid and concise distillation of a political philosophy derived from the Edgar Cayce readings.

"In one reading (3976–8) we are told that it is typical of men to regard power as the necessary precondition for everything. Man's way is to accumulate power— money, fame, numbers—before attempting anything and to regard the lack of power—especially the lack of monetary power—as a reason for delay and inaction. The human tendency is to regard oneself as powerless and ineffective unless backed by elaborate funding, prestigeful endorsers, or numerous supporters.

"This is a mistaken approach, Cayce tells us. We should, instead, start where we are, take in hand what we do have, apply what we know, *not* find fault, *not* find excuses, *not* put off action until tomorrow. (633–5) Those who look upon monetary conditions as a measure of success look in vain. (2897–4) Rather, we should fill the place where we are—and the Lord will open the way. (607–2) Thus, ten may save a city, even a nation, from destruction or may keep the world intact." (633–5)*

*Politics of Hope, A.R.E. Press, 1971, p.6.

Although Dr. Quest is defining a political philosophy for today, the definition is applicable to Israel. Under the monarchy Israel did become organized, and by the time of Solomon it became the wealthiest, most powerful and influential nation in the earth at that time. Yet the very success caused Israel's decline. To maintain the pomp and luxury of the court put a severe strain on the common man who paid the taxes. The inequalities which burgeoned in this climate led to resentments, suspicions, and hatreds between classes. The leaders became accustomed to luxury and blinded by material things. Few were the kings after David who looked forward to a spiritual kingdom. Too many looked backward with covetous eyes on the splendor of the past and sought to wrest whatever wealth they could from their brothers.

After the death of Solomon and the division of the kingdom, Israel steadily declined and made only half-hearted attempts to search for God. Only a few brief respites of unity and stability followed in the centuries between Solomon and the very lowest point in Israel's history, the destruction of Jerusalem, the sacking of the Temple, and national servitude in Babylon.

One wonders if the wealth, luxury, and power of the kingdom were a necessary part of God's plan. However, these are things for which man yearns, and thus the fulfillment of these desires (and the consequences) became a necessary experience in the overall plan.

That is the pattern for man, Cayce tells us, as long as he sets his heart on material things.

Truly did Israel become "like all the other nations."

Chapter 5

The Birth of a Prophet

And it came to pass, in due time Hannah conceived and bore a son and called him Samuel, saying, Because I have asked him of the Lord. (1 Samuel 1:20)

For this, then, is in *every* birth—the possibilities, the glories, the actuating of that influence of that entrance again of god-man into the earth that man might know the way. (262–103)

Every experience recorded in Scripture can become a personal experience, and nowhere is this shown more beautifully in the readings than in the counseling to mothers.

To articulate the concepts in the readings regarding motherhood two new terms have emerged: "Psychic Motherhood" and "Soul Attraction."

Psychic Motherhood and Soul Attraction

Psychic means "of the soul." Psychic forces, the readings tell us, partake of both the mental and spiritual selves and manifest, when conditions are met, through the physical body.

The concept of "psychic motherhood" involves all levels of the self, body, mind, and soul. The view the readings take of motherhood involve concepts relating not only to the reproduction of the physical being, but to the propagation and perpetuation of the best mental and spiritual qualities in a family, race, or nation.

Soul attraction is stated simply in the principle of "like attracts like." There are many souls who are in other dimensions of consciousness outside the earth's sphere. After the Flood, souls could enter into the earth through the natural channels supplied by the sexual union of man and woman.

Since the Fall, when spiritual energy became sexual energy, the descendants of Adam were dedicated to the purification and restoration of man's creative potential.

The readings spoke of the sex urge as being both sacred and a privilege.

Train *him,* train *her,* train *them* rather in the sacredness of that which has come to them as a privilege, which has come to them as a heritage; from a falling away, to be sure, but through the purifying of the body in thought, in act, in certainty, it may make for a people, a state, a nation that may indeed herald the coming of the Lord. (5747-3)

Conception can take place purely through a physical act. The channel which results from this union may attract to it a soul in a low state of spiritual development. Proper dedication will attract a soul in a more advanced state.

Man was given the ability to create through self a channel through which the manifestations of spirit might be made manifest in a material world. As is observed in such, there needs be first that of desire, purpose. It is known as a fact that this may be wholly of the carnal or animal nature on the part of even one, and yet conception may take place; and the end of that physical activity is written in that purpose and desire.

Then it is evident that there is the ideal, as well as the partial or whole carnal force, that may be manifested or exercised in and through such activities—as to bring a channel of mental, spiritual, and material expression in the earth.

The ideal manner, first, is that there may be a channel through which the spirit of truth, hope, divine knowledge and purpose, may be made manifest. (281-46)

The Cayce readings offer a wealth of valuable information on the preparations for parenthood. Physical, mental, and spiritual exercises and disciplines were prescribed. The readings emphasized holding positive mental attitudes before and during pregnancy.

The ideal condition is where there is union of purpose between husband and wife.

Thus the greater unison of purpose, of desire, at a period of conception brings the more universal consciousness—or being—for a perfect or equalized vibration for that conception. (281-46)

By holding the proper ideal and purpose, and with definite expectations of the type and nature of the desired child, prospective parents can, to a large degree, attract to them the type of soul they desire.

In speaking to a five-month-pregnant woman, Cayce said:

The attitude . . . is BEAUTIFUL! And this held, it becomes as that of old—the remembrance of the Creative Forces in their activity with that body that presents itself as a channel for the expression of a soul into the material world . . . *Hope* for, *see*, the son of thine own body becoming as an expression of the love of the heavenly Father in the experience of those that would make His ways their ways; and we will find that such will be the experiences . . .

Q-6. Do I understand that the sex of the child is a boy?

A-6. As has been given, *desire, look for*, a son. (1102-3)

Another young woman, 457, became very interested in the concepts of motherhood as given through Edgar Cayce, and obtained a whole series of readings on them.

In May, 1943, she requested a reading regarding mental and spiritual preparation "for the creation and best development of a child." This was the tenth in a series.

Cayce responded:

In giving information, or in answering questions respecting mental and spiritual attitudes, all of these should be approached from THIS basis of reasoning—especially as preparations are made in body, mind, and spirit for a soul's entrance into the material plane.

While as an individual entity [457] presents the fact of a body, a mind, a soul—it has been given as a promise, as an opportunity to man through coition, to furnish, to create a channel through which the Creator, God, may give to individuals the opportunity of seeing, experiencing His handiwork.

Thus the greater preparations that may be made, in earnest, in truth, in offering self as a channel, is first physical, then the mental attitude; knowing that God, the Creator, will supply that character, that nature may have its course in being and in bringing into material manifestation a soul. For, in being absent from a physical body a soul is in the presence of its Maker.

Then, know the attitude of [the] mind of self, of the companion, in creating the opportunity; for it depends upon the state of attitude as to the nature, the character that may be brought into material experience.

Leave *then* the spiritual aspects to God. Prepare the mental and the physical body, according to the nature, the character of that soul being sought. (457–10)

A very high ideal was found in another young woman, not yet married, who asked:

Q–16. What is the foundation for my great desire in the present life for a child, to give to the world an

offering through a son that would be dedicated to
God?

A–16. It answers itself . . . Retain same, for in the end
this must bring to self a knowledge that all channels,
all vessels of a physical body, may be consecrated in
such a manner to those of the spiritual forces as to
bring forth that seed in due season, in and through
those channels to which they became dedicated to
that service. (288–29)

Prospective parents must make necessary mental and
spiritual preparations to fulfill the high office their sexual
union makes available to them. Union of purpose through
a spiritual ideal results in a more perfectly balanced offspring in the spiritual, mental and physical aspects.

To illustrate the rich possibilities of motherhood,
Cayce referred several young women to the example of
Hannah and Samuel.

Hannah and Samuel

Hannah is revered because she is the mother of the
first great prophet of Israel.

Samuel was an unusual and highly developed soul
who appeared at a critical and difficult stage in Israel's
spiritual development—during the transition from rule
by judges to rule by kings.

He was born during a period of spiritual darkness. At
the time of Samuel's birth, "the word of the Lord was
precious in Israel; there was no open vision." (1 Samuel
3:1) This condition existed, according to Edgar Cayce,
because no one was offering himself as a channel
through which the Spirit could speak.

In thy reading (for ye are a greater interpreter of
books, of writings of others), have ye not wondered
why in the sacred writings it is said that God no longer
spoke to man in visions or dreams?

It is because man fed not his soul, his mind, upon
things spiritual; thus closing the avenue or channel

through which God might speak with the children of men.

For, only they who believe He *is* may make manifest that as a reality in their experience ... (1904-2)

At a time when the word of God was scarce, Samuel received direct guidance. Samuel was recognized early as a prophet of the Lord. Even as a young boy, his words were declared throughout all Israel.

Samuel was the last judge of Israel and the first of the great oral prophets. The Cayce readings state Samuel established a School of Prophets based upon the teaching of Melchizedek. (254-109) The readings locate this school at Carmel (2520-1), although references in the Bible might indicate there were other centers at Ramah, Bethel, Jericho, and Gilgal (1 Samuel 19:20; 2 Kings 2:3, 5; 4:38).

As judge, Samuel was sole director of Israel's welfare from the death of Eli, his predecessor as high priest, to the coronation of Saul. Although not of the priestly tribe of the Levites, Samuel functioned also as the high priest.

He was priest, judge, and prophet in one. Thus Samuel holds a unique position in Jewish history. The synthesis of roles and responsibilities held by Samuel is seen by many commentators as a spiritual foreshadowing of Jesus Christ who represents the final fusing of priest and king.

Thus, at a critical and crucial time in Israel's development, when a great choice was made which was to affect the history and the destiny of this nation dedicated to God, a soul appeared who was equal to the task before it. Without the prayers and dedication of the mother, Hannah, perhaps this incarnation would not have been possible.

An Example

The opening chapter in the first book of Samuel relates the circumstances of the birth of Samuel.

Elkanah, of the tribe of Ephraim, had two wives, Hannah and Pannah. Pannah bore her husband many children, but Hannah, the wife he loved most, bore Elkanah none.

Elkanah was a religious man, and once a year he went to the temple at Shiloh and offered sacrifice. Pannah, because of her fruitful womb, taunted and ridiculed Hannah because Hannah was sterile.

Compassionate Elkanah tried to calm his favored wife. But Hannah could not be consoled.

After many years of being provoked and irritated by Pannah, she went to the temple. From the abundance of her grief and the bitterness in her soul, she wept and lamented while she prayed, supplicating the Lord for a son. She vowed if she conceived she would give him to the Lord.

Eli, the high priest, observed the weeping and wailing woman and thought that she was drunk, but after admonishing her and hearing her story, he assured Hannah her prayers would be answered.

In a short while they were and Hannah was faithful to her vows.

In several instances the readings recommended a study of the story of Hannah. In one reading dedicated solely to information which would help parents develop in their children a complete and integrated expression of the psychic, or soul, forces, Cayce stated in the opening passage:

Well that such rules as were given by Hannah or Elkanah be observed, that there is the consecration of those bodies. (5747-1)

Several aspects already discussed under "psychic motherhood and soul attraction" can be discerned in the story of Hannah.

The love relationship between Hannah and Elkanah would suggest they shared more nearly a union of purpose and ideals.

Like Sarah, Rebekah, and Rachel, Hannah experienced a long period of barrenness. Thus there was a long period of preparation, dedication, and desire. Hannah set forth her reasons for conception.

Finally, conception was viewed as a gift from God and reverenced as such.

Cayce counseled Mrs. 1968 about the need for mothers to prepare for the entry of souls who could meet the difficult and crucial years in the national history which lay ahead. A similiar parallel could be drawn to Hannah and Samuel, and the critical role he filled in a tumultuous and troubled time.

The reading advised a study of Hannah. A lesson on purpose follows.

Thus, as has been indicated and as should be, the entity may in this experience be the mother of those who may fill high places; and there needs be that those who fill high places in the present, and the more so for the days to come, be well grounded in the law of the Lord. For it is perfect and will convert the souls of men.

So in the application of self in the present:

Study first to show thyself in body, in mind, in purpose as one seeking to be a channel of blessings to others, keeping self unspotted from the world, condemning none; and as ye do this, ye may become that channel through which help, understanding, yea, many, many individuals may come to know the Lord. Remember, as ye apply self, read, study how Hannah dedicated herself in body, in mind and gave, not by word, but by activity as well, her son to the glory of God.

As ye practice, as ye apply this in thy experience, ye may set thy face so that thy prayers, thy supplications may be heard, and He will not withhold any good thing from those who seek His coming. Thus, may ye apply in this life thy purposes to become the mother of those who may bless the nation. (1968–10)

Hannah is also an illustration of consecration as well as purpose. Mrs. 457, in one of her early readings, asked:

Q-16. I received a message that next spring I should do my duty in letting a soul incarnate through me. If so, should conception take place now or in the spring?

A-16. Conception should take place when thy body and thy mind, thy companion and his mind, are purified in the light of the desires of thine heart through the exercising of the offices committed into thine keeping through the giver of life who manifests through the sons of men the glories unto God, even as in the Christ. Then, whether this be in December, March, or May, *when* thou hast opened thine mind, thine soul and purified thy body, let *Him* call His own into being through thee!

For, does He prepare the body? Hast thou read how that Hannah blessed not only her household but her peoples and the world by the prayer that her offspring might come from and be a joy unto the Lord all his days?

Dost the Lord prepare the way? Who will say nay? (457-3)

For another, Cayce hearkened to Hannah as an illustration of preparation.

Too oft individuals are too prone to look upon conception or childbirth as purely a physical condition. Rather should it be considered, as it has been from the beginning, that life—[or the] sources of life—is from one source. Oft those who may yearn within their material minds for children are indeed blessed, if they were to consider all the environs to which a soul-entity would have to become accustomed.

Remember how Hannah prepared herself, and how others—as Mary—prepared themselves. There are many recorded, and there are many others of which nothing is heard, and yet there was the long preparation. For God is to each entity, individual. He must become Father-God. For as the Master indicates, "Our Father." He has become this to those who seek to be a channel through which God may bring life for a purpose.

Then make thyself a channel, physically, mentally, spiritually. To be sure, law applies. For in the beginning of man, in His becoming a living soul in the earth, laws were established and these take hold. But lose not sight of the law of grace, the law of mercy, the law of patience as well. For each has its place, especially when individual entities consider and seek, desire, that they be channels through which life, God, may manifest. (2977-2)

A Time of Stress

What are the ideal conditions for bringing a child into this world? The answer must be found in the ideal and purpose for which conception is desired, in the inner-state of the parent, rather than in any external circumstance.

Again, Hannah is a lesson. When she conceived, she was surrounded by those in her own household who taunted and ridiculed her.

For a young woman who had doubts about having children because of material circumstances, Cayce gave the following counsel:

The fact that there has been in the experience of this entity and its companion the mind of doubt, because of material needs and because of mental aspects as may have been or might be a heritage physically, has delayed or prevented such activities. Remember, there is an example of such in the Scripture that the entity would do well to study, to analyze; not merely as a historical fact but the attitude not only of Hannah but of those about the entity who doubted the purpose.

Then, in that same attitude as that entity may this entity in that way bring those activities as may best endow self, as well as the offspring, to be a messenger,

99

a channel to the glory of God and to the honor of self. (457-10)

Not only were there conditions of stress for Hannah in her own household, but also in the nation and the world about her.

The Philistines were firmly settled along the coastal plain of southern Canaan, and were intent upon the conquest of all Canaan. From their sweep through Asia Minor they had wrested the secret of iron smelting from the Hittites, the first iron founders in the world. Thus, the Philistines were a well seasoned, experienced, first-class military machine, equipped with weapons far superior to those of Israel. (1 Samuel 13:19-20)

The priests of Shiloh could offer little or nothing for the uplift and edification of the people. God spoke no longer in dreams or open vision. Hophni and Phineas, the sons of Eli the high priest, were notorious profligates who reviled and abused the women of the congregation and forced offerings from the men.

In further counseling Mrs. 457, Cayce described a similarity of needs in Hannah's time and in the present.

Q-1. Is it right to being a child into being in a world such as we have today, even though it may never know a normal life but only one of war and killing and anger and hate?

A-1. The doubt as created in self, from the very asking of such a question, may be answered best in considering the attitude, the conditions which existed in those people's minds and activities at the period given as an example. If that does not answer, then to this entity it cannot be answered . . .

Q-4. Should I read any books for my spiritual development besides *A Search for God*?

A-4. Read the Book of all books—especially Deuteronomy 30, and Samuel—considering especially the attitude of Hannah, the conditions, the circumstances which existed not only as to its relationship to its husband and to other companions, but as to the needs for spiritual awakening in that experience—which exist in the world and the earth today. (457-10)

Obviously taking the lessons of Samuel and Hannah to heart, in her eleventh reading 457 asked:

Q-25. Hannah turned over her first son to a priest to bring up. Is that feasible today or should I try to bring him up in the way of God myself?
A-25. This must be dependent upon the body itself. The conditions and circumstances surrounding such to-day are not the same as in those periods. But there may be those administrations, or the giving over of the body at those periods such as Samuel was given, for complete education; which is indicated in certain types of schools that are organized throughout the land in the present. (457-11)

The Shadow of Jealousy

Both Samuel and Eli, his teacher, shared a similar fate regarding their children. Eli's sons were notorious. Samuel's first prophetic message was about the destruction these two sons had brought upon the house of Eli. Samuel's sons were not of his character either. They perverted justice and took bribes. The Israelites grew increasingly disturbed by the fact that, after Samuel's death, they would be judged by these two sons. This provided the people with a reason—or excuse—for demanding a king.

"So often we have seen cases where the parents were good, Christian people, who did everything they could to bring up their children properly and yet they turned out badly," Edgar Cayce said to his Bible class. "Why? The answer, or an example may be found in the experience of Hannah and Samuel."

The answer is found in the information in the readings regarding "psychic motherhood." Not only do the ideals and purposes affect the character of the child, but also the attitudes and emotions of the parents, especially the mother.

Then, know the attitude of mind of self, of the companion, in creating the opportunity [for a soul to manifest]; for it depends upon the state of attitude as to the nature, the character that may be brought into material experience. (457–10)

It is known as a fact that [the desire] may be wholly of the carnal or animal nature ... and yet conception may take place; and the end of that physical activity is written in that purpose and desire.

Then it is evident that there is the ideal, as well as the partial or whole carnal force, that may be manifested or exercised in and through such activities—as to bring a channel of mental, spiritual, and material expression in the earth. (281–46)

The 281 series of readings, devoted to an interpretation of the Revelation of St. John and healing prayer, contains a section devoted to "psychic motherhood." In the forty-seventh reading in the series, Cayce traced the connection between Rachel's feeling of superiority throughout her period of gestation and young Joseph's haughty attitude toward his brothers. In the same series Hannah was also used as an illustration of the negative consequences inherited by the son from the wrong attitudes of the mother.

When Hannah desired that there be an expression that God, the Universal Consciousness, had not forgotten that there were prayers and alms offered, was there wholly the lack of selfishness? or was there the shadow of jealousy?

Then we find there was the promise of the dedication and the purposes, that this expression would be wholly given to the Lord, ever. Yet it brought into being an entity, though dedicated as few—yea, as none other individually—to the Lord—unable of himself to give that in expression which would keep his own offspring in the SAME vibration [of dedication]! (281–47)

Edgar Cayce amplified this concept in his lectures to the Bible class.

"Although Hannah made a promise to the Lord and kept it, we can see quite a bit of selfishness in her first prayer. [1 Samuel 2:1–10] Her greatest desire was not that she should bring a prophet into the world, but that she should be given a son in order to silence those who were taunting her. She was filled with jealousy toward Elkanah's other wife. Even in her song of thankfulness, we can see her attitude of rebuking those who had acted arrogantly toward her. Outwardly she was saying, 'See what the Lord has done,' while inwardly, no doubt, she was exalting in her triumph over Pannah.

"This is a human trait, of which we all are guilty. But we can see the effect of this in Samuel's life—in his inability to control his own sons."

Selfishness entered into Hannah's prayer, and it might be said that a certain amount of self-centeredness existed in Samuel. He was the superior soul Hannah longed for, and Samuel kept to those things in which he excelled. His primary preoccupation was with God and the nation. Perhaps it never occurred to him that he should give the same attention to the needs of his family.

The Cayce readings stress the importance of *balance*. All aspects of life—God, man, and family—should be considered as One. The first commandment indicates perfect love is when God, neighbor, and self are loved equally.

While setting a high standard for his children, Samuel failed to give them the proper attention and instruction. Thus a reaction set in. As is so often the case, the children not only lacked the desire to live up to their father's standards, but rebelled and did exactly the opposite of everything he wished.

The failure, or inability, of Samuel and Eli to direct their sons (an experience of countless parents) raises a question of spiritual training. When should it begin? Cayce pondered this with his students.

"We wonder why it was that Eli's sons and Samuel's turned out so badly, when they themselves lived the best they knew and tried in every way to do the will of God and fulfill their offices as priest and prophet.

"Perhaps it was because Eli and Samuel did not start soon enough with their sons' spiritual development. Possibly this should have begun before their birth. This we would gather, even from Hannah's experience."

The foundation for this philosophy was expressed in a reading nine years before this discussion took place in the Bible class. In June, 1932, a reading was given "How to Develop Your Psychic Powers." It was requested by Edgar Cayce himself in preparation for a lecture for the first A.R.E. congress.

Study as to how Hannah consecrated the life of her son to the service of Jehovah, how that he was under the influence of the law in every respect and tutored by one who was unable to (or did not, at least) tutor his own. What was the difference? The consecration of the body yet unborn! When would one begin, then, to teach or train children? Many months even before there is the conception, that the influence is *wholly* of the Giver of good and perfect gifts. (5752-2)

Leave THEN the spiritual aspects God. (457-10)

Although his inability to pass on his sense of purpose and dedication to his own sons may appear as a failure or shortcoming in Samuel, Samuel did fulfill the purpose for which he incarnated into the earth. He was a true prophet and judge. Under his influence, Israel threw off the yoke of Philistine domination. Samuel paved the way for the organization of the kingdom under David. This, perhaps, was his main mission. Yet one cannot discount the importance of the School of Prophets which he founded. It exerted a tremendous influence upon the rest of Israel's history, and eventually became the Essene movement.

Thus it can be said confidently, Samuel did the will of God, even if his sons did not.

Mrs. 457, in the eleventh in her series on preparing for motherhood, was obviously referring to the example of Hannah in the 281 readings, when she asked:

Q-26. Where is the first failure which brought about such men as Samuel and Isaac ... (457-11)

Edgar Cayce interrupted her in mid-question, and retorted:

Not a failure; it is being wholly in accord with God's purposes with the individual. Man expects to have God to work according to man's idea as to when. God takes His time. (457-11)

Her next question was a resumption of the first.

Q-27. Was it in the original conception of Samuel and Isaac or in their upbringing afterwards?
A-27. As has been indicated, these were dedicated to the Lord, God. HIS time is not man's time. This is indicated in the birth of Isaac, also in the birth of Samuel. For there is little or nothing that changed the pathological effects in the life or experience of Hannah after the birth of Samuel. It was purely, then, a physical condition. But having dedicated, having promised those things to God—God's promises to man, in God's own time—these were fulfilled. The same as they were with Samson, as well as with Isaac and Samuel. (457-11)

Mother of the Prophet
Hannah Reincarnated

On January 22, 1938, a young couple obtained a life reading for their week-old daughter. The father was deeply involved with the study of metaphysics and is author of several books on the spiritual life.

The father's background and the information in the child's Life Reading suggest the attraction of kindred spirits.

The reading stated the child was exceptional and described several important incarnations. In the opening passage, Cayce gave the first surprising intimations of its past lives.

Also it is indicated that the entity is one of a very DETERMINED nature, one that will go to extremes oft—or there is the inclination—to have its OWN way.

One that will be inclined to judge, gauge, or measure its activities in every phase of experience by the material gains or material accomplishments of the entity.

Hence the spiritual lessons, the spiritual natures and inclinations MUST be developed; though from the activities of the entity in the material plane one from the material angle would wonder how, WHY the entity could EVER be material-minded in the present! when it was a prophetess as Anna, when it was the MOTHER of the PROPHET as Hannah! ...

When the records here as we find are considered, the name should be Mary Hannah or Mary Anna; as this HAS been the name of the entity that is expressed or manifested in this body ... (1521-1)

New and subtle dimensions of interest accrue when Life Readings contain incarnations of personages who are familiar to us either through secular or religious history. A study of history shows how an individual affected the development of a state, a nation, or mankind, while the reading shows the overall understanding the soul has of the Spirit, and shows how the soul developed in lives preceding its advent into history, and the wisdom in which it spent its energies in succeeding lives.

1521-1 is an unusual reading in that it contains three lives which are preserved in our literature, and demonstrates a continuity of moral and spiritual development.

In her previous life she had been Ann Boleyn, the

second wife of King Henry VIII and mother of Queen Elizabeth, ". . . or that one who lost in its attempt to hold *to* those forces and influences that would *hold* to its religion and its moral life"; in the life before Ann Boleyn, she had been Anna the prophetess (Luke 2:36–39) who suffered in mind and body for a spiritual ideal; and before that she had been Hannah, the mother of Samuel.

In the opening passage, Cayce warned the parents that 1521 would have tendency to judge its activities by the material gains or accomplishments it would bring.

Cayce warned the parents again about her materialistic strain as he described that notable incarnation as Hannah.

. . . we find the entity was in the earth during those periods when the children of promise were in the lands of promise, when the preparations and the settlements and the changes had been wrought.

And though there were those individuals and groups who forsook the counsel of Joshua and Moses, the entity then—as Hannah—made overtures for that promise; and it was THAT entity [Samuel] that was HOPED, that was visioned, that might have been a part of the experience! And yet it may be the guiding force of THIS entity through this sojourn, if there are those activities of those about the entity in the matter of the spiritual guidance that this entity may be dedicated to the spiritual laws and not material things alone.

As Hannah the entity gained throughout in those activities. And though ever looked upon by those in a material experience as one apart, one separate, the entity gained the experience of knowing that God in his heavens does take thought, does take cognizance of the prayers, of the supplications, of the activities of an individual that are in accordance with the manner and way the individual prays.

To that experience may the entity harken for its great awakening. (1521–1)

Two Spiritual Guides
Elkanah and Samuel

A spiritual guide is an unincarnated entity who is acting as a benevolent influence in the safeguarding and development of a soul in the earth. The readings indicate that souls who are "in-between" earthly lives, act as "guardian angels."

The readings also speak about souls who have never incarnated into the flesh, who project mental and spiritual forces into the earth for the uplift and benefit of man. These are spoken of as "the hierarchies" or "guardians of the Realm."

Elkanah, Hannah's husband and father of Samuel, was designated as a spiritual guide for a forty-six-year-old business executive.

Q-1. Please give name and history of highest spirit guide assigned to my wife and me?
A-1. These had best be sought in self. Not that these may not be given, for they are present with thee in thy activities; but "What is thy name?" that has been sought by others, and as the answer came then, "What meanest these experiences in thy life?" so may the name come to thee, even as it did to Elkanah as he offered the sacrifice, as he offered meat—for he is thy guide.
Q-2. Has he any instructions as for our contact with him?
A-2. Seek and ye shall find. Put into application that thou knowest day by day, for it is line upon line, precept upon precept, here a little and there a little that ye gather together those forces that make for the greater material manifestation of those influences in thy daily experience that may bring thee to the consciousness, to the understanding of those forces that would aid thee.

For, as has been given, when thou hast shown in thine heart thy willingness to be guided and directed by *His* force, He gives His angels charge concerning thee that they bear thee up and prevent the stumblings that come to the sons of the Creative Forces in and among the sons of men.

Hence keep—keep—true to self and to that thou knowest, for the way is open before thee. Seek rather to show thyself as one worthy of acceptance to the God-influence that is shown in man's experience through the manifestations of His Son in the earth; for He is thy guide; *He* will show thee the way. His brethren, His brothers in the activities in the earth, may show thee thy way.

Q-3. What is the sign of His presence?

A-3. The circle with the Cross; these make for the sign that all thou hast heard is fulfilled in Him. (423-3)

In the Life Reading for 1521, an intimation was given that Samuel was acting as the spiritual guide for 1521. A second reading was given eighteen months later. Although requested for physical reasons, the reading elaborated on the spiritual relationship in the present between Samuel and the baby. The reading suggests the continuity of an enduring spiritual relationship and ends with a prophecy that infers the child might again be the mother of a prophet.

... a drop more often than one drop, you see; and this would be given about twice each week ... This as we find ... will purify the glandular system as to resist adverse influences; combined, of course, with those directions under that influence as may come from Samuel—through the prayer. (1521-2)

During the period of pregnancy, Edgar Cayce had a conscious vision of the expected child being a male.

The next question was asked about the change in sex.

Q-6. Is the soul which is/was hoped might come in the place of this entity, and as a male, that which was Samuel, the son of Hannah?

A–6. As indicated, as outlined, the prayer to and through the guiding force of Samuel will aid in the help to Samuel's mother.

Q–7. If so, is this the soul which will aid the entity and to which the entity can pray for guidance?

A–7. As just indicated. This has been indicated before; it is indicated here.

For, as some would have it, the hierarchies are not unmindful of the developing of souls through the experiences in the earth. Hence such is not OUT of the ordinary, but the natural spiritual development in and through the very association and the prayer and care of those to whom such a soul is entrusted.

For, as has been indicated, there is—to be sure—something of a choice of the entity seeking expression. In the material world and materiality, it is more often trained or convinced *away* from its natural spiritual import. For, is it not for spiritual development that each soul enters? and not merely for mental OR material or physical?

For in the pattern, which is the way and the manner, we find that these phases are ever considered as one; yet the Mother [Mary] kept these and pondered them in her heart.

What meaneth this? save as to that injunction which would be given to every parent: Ponder well the expressions that arise from the emotions of a developing child; for, as has been forever given, train them in the way they should go and when they are old they will not depart from the way.

Q–8. Explain why the change of entity and the change of sex took place, between the time when a son was indicated through this channel, on September 23, 1937, and the birth of the child.

A–8. This, as has been indicated, was given that there might be the greater opportunity for the developing of the entity Hannah UNDER the direction of Samuel, with the aid AND direction of thought by the parents. This was deemed by the seeker as the channel for expression. (1521–2)

The last answer ends with a clairvoyant's prediction.

Q–9. What is the mission of the entity in this experience?

A–9. That the glory of the Father in the Son may be the more magnified in the lives of those the entity meets.

As the entity brought into the experience of a peoples a new form, a new character of a determining factor between the peoples and the worship of the living God, so may the entity in this experience bring into experience—through the preparation of its body, its mind for the creating or bringing into conception— an activity that may, AS the son then, again revolutionize that relationship of man to the awareness of his relationship to God.

For the offspring of this entity will anoint a holy one! (1521–2)

The closing statement raises an intriguing possibility. The soul has, as Ann Boleyn and Hannah, been a mother to those who have filled high places. The readings suggests this pattern will repeat itself. Perhaps Samuel will incarnate through her again in this life.

There is an interesting footnote to this prophecy in the case file. On July 26, 1965, 1521 reported in a letter to Gladys Davis Turner, Edgar Cayce's secretary, that she was the mother of a precocious sixteen-month-old boy. "Even allowing for the natural prejudice of parents," she wrote, "it is clear that he is an unusual child . . . He stands up for his own rights and goes his own way . . . He remembers everything . . . He is a constant source of amazement to us and all who meet him."

She reported three years later she had given birth to a second son.

Chapter 6

The Story of Saul

If, as the readings suggest, the Bible is the story of the unfoldment of Man in the earth, each phase in this pattern is advanced, not by the evolution of the people as a whole, but through individuals. Evolution, the readings tell us, is not a collective phenomenon, but occurs on an individual basis, through the gradual overcoming of self.

God created souls to be companions and co-creators with Him. His relationship with His children was always meant to be personal and direct. But as souls separated, they put many things between them and their creator. In the beginning, the first temptation was to partake of the tree of knowledge. Self-indulgence and complete disregard for spiritual laws brought on the Deluge. At Babel, the Sons of God turned again to material things, which resulted in the dispersion of tongues, a further fragmentation of the original oneness.

Now, at the time of Samuel, Israel was entering a new phase in their involvement with materiality. They were again being tempted with material things.

Reading 440-4 states that the highest psychic realization which can come to man is "that God, the Father, speaks directly to the sons of men." Direct experience and personal contact and guidance from the Highest is the cornerstone and foundation upon which the nation of Israel was established.

During the Exodus, the Israelites were content for

Joshua and Moses to meet with God and relay His messages. They were willing to listen, but when the time came to apply those truths by going in and possessing the promised land, they lacked that confirming and energizing contact with the Spirit which comes through direct experience. They balked and were terrified, and a long period of wandering began.

Now once again, Israel lacked the confidence to leave destiny in God's hands. They wanted a man to rule them, a king who would "go out before us and fight our battles." (1 Samuel 8:20)

In the broadest sense, the figure of a king symbolizes the universal and archetypal Man. Any man may properly be called a king, when his life reaches its culminating point. Thus, the first king of Israel, a nation which symbolizes the story of man, was given a unique opportunity. In a new era of evolution, he could set the ideal and hold a light which would establish a model of man's own potential.

The Monarchy was part of God's Plan: a natural development if the people had been patient. David would have arisen to weld Israel into one whole, supplying it with its greatest impetus for immortality throughout the national history. The whole experience with Saul could have been avoided had not the monarchy been forced into premature birth.

Yet, beginning with the episode between Sarah, Hagar, and Abraham, the history of Israel is filled with forced issues with God.

The readings tell us the fruits of an act can rise no higher than the source from which they emanate. Rather than waiting for a king to be given them "in God's own time," the people demanded one of their own. The source of their demand was not founded in the Promises of the past, but in their fear, greed, and unbelief in the present. These seeds reaped their own harvest. Saul, like the people who demanded him, did not transcend his own human nature.

Only by the deepest devotion and use of his will power could Saul have set the example which Israel needed held before them. Yet the two features which Saul needed most were exactly those lacking, as a life reading will show us.

"Head and Shoulders Above the Rest"

The threat posed by the eminently well-organized and powerful Philistines created in at least one Israelite couple, Kish and Methulabah, the parents of Saul, the desire for a son who would be their nation's deliverer.

Kish and Methulabah prepared themselves mentally and physically before conception took place. This had an effect on the developing embryo. The result was shown in the physical stature of Saul who was "head and shoulders above the rest." (1 Samuel 10:23)

Although his mental and physical attributes came as a birthright through the parents, Saul, later in life, used these endowments selfishly.

. . . in those relationships borne by Kish and Methulabah, when there were the preparations for the individual entity that was to be king over that chosen people. We find that the preparation of the parents, mentally and physically, was such that there was an elongation of activity in the endocrine system of the pineal [in the embryo] so that the stature of the entity then was of a different type, a different nature, and the mental and spiritual so balanced and coordinated that through the experience of the entity there was a physical and mental development equaled and surpassed by few.

Yet the APPLICATION of the entity *of* those opportunities was personal; so that what was individually personified of the mental and spiritual of the entity's sojourn was then of self in its *latter* analysis. (281–49)

Saul was conceived in righteous desire, yet was unable to hold to his own religious convictions.

Neither is it easy to understand the illustrations used from the life of Kish, who conceived through righteous desire a son, a channel chosen for a manifestation of material power in a material world; given through the choice of the Maker Himself, and yet the INDIVIDUAL in his personal relationships defied even that which had been prophesied by himself! (281–51)

The destiny of an individual is not determined by the forces of heredity and environment but, as the readings stress, through the use of his Free Will in relation to his development of the God-given abilities which are latent and manifest in his soul.

Then, it is not that the entire life experience is laid out for an individual when there has been received that imprint as of the first breath or the spirit entering the body as prepared for activity in the material world. For, again, choice is left to the individual, and the personality—as to whether it is the laudation of the ego or cooperation with its fellow men, or as a consecration to the service of the Creative Forces in its material environs. (281–49)

Thus the following is a succinct summation of the life of Saul.

Q–1. Is the following statement true or false: Saul, the son of righteous Kish, in the latter part of his life chose evil. It was the exercising of his own choice rather than environmental or hereditary conditions.
A–1. Correct. (281–54)

The Leader They Deserved

It is a familiar principle in politics (and metaphysics) that "the people get the leader they deserve." No man rises to power save that he speaks to the collective needs and beliefs of the majority he governs.

One reading tells us Samuel introduced a new factor in the relationships between the people and their worship of God. This new concept is expressed by Samuel in 1 Samuel 12:13–15.

It indicates the people bear the responsibility for their leaders. The power still rests with the people. Their relationship is still directly between God and them. But now there is an "intervening" factor.

If the people do good, the king will do good. If the people are evil, the king will not rise above it. Yet, if the people want to do good, and the king refuses, then the people have the right to change him.

A new factor of conscience and responsibility is laid upon the people.

On November 27, 1923, a young Oklahoma oil promoter obtained a physical reading from Edgar Cayce. In the reading, the man was described, in part, as follows.

Is this "the leader they deserved"?

One spiritually high-minded. Physically weak in developing much of that condition. One given to do a great deal towards [the] uplift of man, when used properly. *Not always done*. One given to control men through the mental. Not always controlled properly. One given to create a balance, and to find the equalizing forces with the masses. *Not always used properly*.

Be better physically, mentally, if this were kept in the straight and narrow forces than [it] has been at times. (221–1)

The accuracy of this reading inspired the man to write Edgar Cayce, requesting a life reading.

In the second reading, three weeks following, the young man was told he had been Saul, Israel's first king!

Although the opening passage is a description of the present state of the entity's development, much that is in it is applicable to Saul.

This life reading is among the earliest given by Edgar Cayce.

Edgar Cayce: Yes, we have the body, the conditions here, and the records as has been made, and as will be made, both in the present and past and future ... All is not good, yet in many phases of earth's sphere, known as success, this individual will rise high, yet ever those of the wandering forces, as gained from the influence of the Mercury and Neptune forces, will be in this entity's doing and undoing ... Saturn and Mars afflicting, Moon's forces being earth's spheres. Hence the entity's ability to handle those forces in nature that come from earth's storehouse, and any of the elements of this nature become the speculative forces for financial returns to this body in the earth plane ... One with the afflictions of the forces as given in Mars and Saturn will and does make one slow to wrath, but subtle in the ultraextent in carrying out purposes, good or bad.

One that in the greater development will find moments, hours, years of sublime forces entering in with the great vision of Venus and Jupiter forces, yet holding these rather as ideals than making of these forces a reality in his own experience.

Those of the Moon and Sun's forces we find working as antagonistic in the development of financial forces in Mercurian elements, yet one that will oft times have within his grasp the higher influences of financial force in [the] earth plane.

As to forces with the will as established in self, the entity would do well to keep in that straight and narrow way that leadeth to life everlasting, giving of itself in the moments and hours of the Jupiterian force as is found in the next five months ... (221–2)

Although in later years in other readings, (5148–2 and 281–48) Cayce attributed Seth (Genesis 5:3) and Benjamin (Genesis 35:18), respectively, as earlier incarnations of Saul, in this life reading neither of the two are mentioned:

In the personalities of the individual we find as obtained from these conditions:

Before this we find this portion of entity in that of the Grecian age when the fall of the government was under the rule of the idealists and the materialists became the ruling force of the day. This entity, as then, was the leading force in the minority at the time; hence was often referred to as the weakling of the day.

In that before we find the entity as that of the leader [Saul] as chosen for the first king in and with the chosen people, and was the herder as sought the lost animals of his father when appointed as the leader.

Hence we find in this present sphere those elements bringing through in this personality and individuality those as in this:

In the first the one chosen of the higher elements. Hence ever those forces about this entity where, though all others fail, this one may, through direct self-control, gain those forces of the higher and highest realms in the present plane.

In the second that force as is manifested in the great thoughts and ideals builded about self, yet ever just beyond carrying those to execution. May be done by sheer will and by adhering to those immutable laws that give self the insight of the forces that lend to the upbuilding of all force relative to the higher elements.

In stature from that of all force, as is given, ever has the entity been under the influence of Mercurian elements. (221-2)

When the Bible class reached the appropriate place in their study of the Book of Samuel, Edgar Cayce quoted extensively from this reading in one discussion. When he concluded with the lessons from the reading, he summed up with the following comment.

"This individual, as you can see from the above, has a very brilliant mind and is very capable, yet lives by his wits, trying to 'outsmart' the next guy.

"If he continues in this direction, he will come up against a brick wall, and have to start all over again, because—by the natural, spiritual laws of the universe —he must comply with the laws of love and universality of purpose.

"Some of us take a long time to learn by experience. We must hit rock bottom before we realize we are headed in the wrong direction."

Saul's Past Lives

Few things happen by chance. No man rises to authority over a nation except by "the grace of God." (5142–1) Any man who is in a commanding position above his brothers has earned that privilege and responsibility by developments in past lives.

As a soul, Saul had been bound up with the ideals and purposes of Israel from the beginning. If the readings are correct, this soul had also manifested as Seth and Benjamin, experiences which, no doubt, prepared him for the privilege of being Israel's first king.

While in the clairvoyant state, Edgar Cayce must have observed an unusual panorama of history. Time and again the readings create subtle and sensitive connections between widely separated happenings. Yet when they are pointed out, the clarity of repeated patterns are discerned.

Thus we find Seth, the third child of Adam and Eve and *first* in the pageant of lineal descent, reincarnated as Saul, *first* among the monarchs of Israel.

There was no self-seeking as Seth. The entity continued his line and successfully advanced the Adamic influence on the earth. As Saul, he was given a similar opportunity, but failed.

This reading draws the lesson.

In giving the interpretations of the records here, there are those experiences in the earth which stand out beyond others, not beyond the present which may be attained, but beyond some others. These may answer questions for some, as to why individuals apparently are so far advanced in one experience and then fail so miserably in others. Self enters in and is ever present. For there is continually, as is set forth in the admonitions of the lawgiver, set before thee today, now and every day good, evil, life and death. Choose thou.

Consider for the moment . . . how that God himself chose Saul as a goodly king, head and shoulders above his fellow men, his countenance that was indeed kingly and gifted with prophecy; and yet he allowed himself because of an exalted physical position to forget his humbleness before God, even as there had been in his experiences in the earth before, in those days as a son of Adam, who had been given that privilege of being the channel through which the chosen of the peoples were to be Abraham, Isaac, and Jacob. (5148–2)

Throughout the reading for 221 (Saul), Cayce called the entity to the greater use of his will and for exercising direct self-control, in order to gain "those forces of the . . . highest realms in the present plane." Beneficent astrological influences fill the mind with sublime vision, yet the thoughts and ideals built by self are "ever just beyond carrying out."

The lack of desire to make the spiritual manifest has long been in the makeup of this soul. It was this vibration in Jacob and Rachel that attracted the soul in its incarnation as Benjamin.

The material love was just as great [as when Joseph had been conceived], the satisfying of material desire was completely fulfilled; yet it lacked that desire to BRING such as was wholly a channel through which the SPIRITUAL was to be made manifest. But it was a channel that EVENTUALLY brought the material made manifest in Saul, an incarnation of Benjamin. (281-48)

If Saul had been Benjamin, then he was the same soul whom Jacob spoke of as "a ravenous wolf." (Genesis 49:27)

Although Saul brought certain weaknesses and short-comings with him in his material incarnation, when he was anointed by Samuel he became a changed man, as the prophet foretold. God "gave him a new heart." (1 Samuel 10:9) However, Saul soon reverted to old habits.

Edgar Cayce saw a hidden significance in the familiar story of Saul's first meeting with Samuel. (1 Samuel 9)

"Saul came to Samuel through the law of material things. His first request from Samuel was material in nature. He wanted Samuel to tell him where his father's asses were.

"Throughout his life, Saul never failed to recognize that Samuel *could* give him the information he sought, but he did fail to use it for the glory of God.

"The spirit of the Lord fell upon Saul, and he prophesied. But only for a short while. The rest of the time he continued to seek his own ends."

What Saul prophesied has not been recorded. Apparently he was flooded with those sublime forces and vision which are, as in the present, "ever just beyond carrying to execution."

... and yet the INDIVIDUAL in his personal relationships defied even that which had been prophesied by himself! (281-51)

Edgar Cayce drew more lessons on Saul for his Bible class.

"If you are once convinced in spirit, or by the Spirit, then God is with you. If you are able to continually

121

hold to that, nothing can go wrong. But if you forget and entertain the spirit of evil, then you know, as Jesus said, 'Your Father is one who can be touched by your infirmities.' Yes, and he can also be touched by your hardness of heart and your negligence.

"We are co-creators with God. Saul had been ordained. He prophesied. He had been convinced in spirit, but he did not hold to it.

"Saul merited the opportunity which was given to him, just as all those who are in power today have earned the position they occupy. What an individual does with his opportunities is between him and God. Nothing can separate you from God's love except yourself.

"We think certain people are destined for certain things. EVERYONE is destined at some time to be a Caesar, to be a Jesus, to be a devil if that's what he wants to be. Everyone has the opportunity to make choices. It is always up to the individual.

"It has been said when the pupil is ready, the teacher appears. If it takes ten lives to accomplish a spiritual purpose, what does it matter. What difference does it make? The main thing is to keep on trying—which is what Saul failed to do!"

The Sin of Saul

The words of Paul to the Hebrews are applicable to Saul:

For it is impossible to restore again to repentance those who have once been enlightened, who have tasted the heavenly gift, and have become partakers of the Holy Spirit, and have tasted the goodness of the word of God and the powers of the age to come, if they then commit apostasy ... (Hebrews 6:4–6)

When Samuel anointed Saul as king, Saul became a changed man. He was filled with the Holy Spirit and prophesied. After receiving the Spirit, he united Israel against the Ammonites, who were threatening the brother tribe of Ephraim. So caught up in the Spirit was he after this victory, he took no credit to himself, but acknowledged it totally as the work of God. So complete and all-possessing was his experience that there was no room within him for vindictiveness or malice toward the Israelites who doubted and despised him. (1 Samuel 11:12–13)

Yet Saul, after partaking of the fullness of the Spirit, failed to produce further Spiritual fruits.

And, as has been given by the lawgiver of old, think not who will descend from heaven to bring you a message; for, Lo, it is already in thine own heart. It is thyself, thy inner self, thy soul self. Think not who will come over the waters, nor over the seas to bring a message, for it is with thee already.

To be sure, these may be encouraged, abetted, kept in line; but it is within self that this must be accomplished. Then if it is used to that of self-indulgence, self-gratification, self-attaining for that of self alone, it becomes sin—even as the sin of Saul. (2995–1)

Saul's Decline
The First Mistake

Shortly after his inspired victory over the Ammonites, (1 Samuel 11) and his magnanimous example of forgiveness, (1 Samuel 11:13) Saul began to show the pattern that would characterize the rest of his reign.

Saul was in the position to set a new ideal for man in his spiritual evolution, and in the second year of his authority he failed his first test. (1 Samuel 13)

After a successful engagement with the Philistines, Saul called for Samuel to prepare a burnt offering. Samuel set a period of seven days as preparation for the ritual. During that time the Philistines began to amass their forces again. Many of the Israelites began to panic and desert. Those who remained with Saul began to waver. But the time of waiting had not passed, and

Samuel did not appear. On the seventh day, Samuel still had not come, and Saul in order to prevent further defections offered the sacrifice himself, thus violating the law of Moses and usurping the sacrosanct privilege of high priest.

Just as he finished the sacrifice, Samuel appeared and rebuked Saul for failing to honor God's laws. This had been a crucial test. Had he proved himself, the Lord would have established Saul forever (13:13). Samuel put Saul on notice that God had chosen a new man, "one after his own heart." (13:14)

Edgar Cayce, who was keenly aware of the importance of attitudes and emotions, saw other indications in this story of Saul's weakness.

"How very much this reminds us of situations in our own lives today. We begin to get panicky and can't wait long enough for the Lord to work through us. We try and figure out a way to do it ourselves. Saul had a good excuse from the material angle. The people were becoming scattered and going home, so he had to hold them by asking for a sacrifice to be brought. He told Samuel he didn't want to go ahead, but forced himself to do it for fear there would be no one left to fight.

"Samuel rebuked him, and from that time on Saul could not take any more rebuke or criticism. He continued to feel his own self-importance more and more, and to exercise his authority more and more arbitrarily."

Saul's Rash Vow

Saul's second mistake was almost a tragic one for his son Jonathan. This episode is recounted in 1 Samuel 14.

Jonathan and his armor bearer engaged the Philistine garrison at Michmash in a night attack. The Philistines, caught by surprise, retreated, thinking Saul's army had attacked. Saul, roused by the sound of battle, marshaled his troops and led them into combat. At the onset he issued a senseless order that, on penalty of death, all his men abstain from eating until he was completely avenged on the Philistines. It would mean almost twenty-four hours without food. Jonathan, unaware of this command, late in the day ate a honeycomb.

When this news was brought to Saul, he found himself trapped by his own rash vow, unable to retract it and loath to carry it out.

The situation is similar to the story of Jephthah (Judges 11), but with a different ending. The people recognized God had been with Jonathan, and stood up for him against Saul. They wouldn't allow Saul to repeat Jephthah's tragic mistake.

"Perhaps Jephthah's daughter could have been saved," Edgar Cayce said, "had the people responded in the same way." This shows the people were beginning to think for themselves, Cayce said, and had remembered what Samuel told them—that they could make the king do what was right.

Although Jonathan escaped an early death this time, he died a young man in battle with Saul. Saul's actions eventually destroyed his whole household.

The King's Son

Two weeks after the reading for the oil promoter who had been King Saul, a successful Dayton, Ohio, real estate broker obtained his life reading. In it he was told that he had been Jonathan, Saul's son, whose friendship with David has been a model of honor and loyalty throughout the ages.

The reading tells us that his life as Jonathan was one of several in which the entity experienced sudden death.

> We find in those forces as has been manifest in the entity's sojourn upon the planes that there have been several sudden deaths, or removal. Hence, the innate feeling that is exhibited that some such condition might possibly happen in the present. (4219-3)

It also comments on the positive developments in the use of his will.

> ... the will with the present entity's development will go far to assist in presenting this entity wholly and acceptable unto Him who giveth all things ... Keep the body fit, that the will and the soul forces may manifest, for the body means much to all who contact same ... (4219-3)

Then with the characteristic briefness of these earliest Life Readings, Edgar Cayce described three unusual and outstanding incarnations.

> As to the personalities as expressed, the individuality as brought from those before:
> The one before this we find in that of the king's son, and the counselor and friend of the shepherd king when the shepherd became king—Jonathan.
> In that before, we find in that of Poseida, when Alta ruled the earth's forces, and was then in that [name] of Aramus.
> In the one before, we find in the early dawn when the forces showed the Sons coming together for the Glory of the earth's plane.
> In the personalities as shown in the present it is in the first [experience] that of the love of sincerity.
> In the second, and in that the life [was] lost in the volcano eruption; in that we find the present forces of judgment of structural forces.
> In the next, the friendship of those who are the faithful to any cause that is just. (4219-3)

Edgar Cayce made these additional remarks about Jonathan to the Bible class.

> "Jonathan was a God-fearing man. Evidently he must have been conceived and born during the early days of Saul's reign, when Saul was still consecrated. We might say Jonathan's mother was a God-fearing woman who later lost favor with Saul through some

disagreements with his plans. When Jonathan was pleading for David, Saul lost his temper and called him, 'Thou son of the perverse, rebellious woman.'

"Jonathan was not selfish or egotistical. He realized Saul was not carrying out Samuel's directions. This fact, with David's character, established a bond of friendship that was out of the ordinary. David, when he was acclaimed a hero, still proclaimed his loyalty to Saul. This drew Jonathan closer to David."

The Third Mistake

The third indication of Saul's poor judgment is recounted in Chapter 15.

Samuel ordered Saul to completely exterminate the Amalekites, thus fulfilling an injunction which had been in effect since the time of Moses. Saul defeated the Amalekites, but he did not completely carry out Samuel's command. He spared King Agag and the best sheep, cattle, and spoil for a sacrifice. Although Saul's intentions may have been good, he demonstrated again, by hedging on Samuel's instructions, he would not hesitate to put his will above God's will, his way above God's way.

To sacrifice is noble, though its intent was probably selfish. After the sacrifice, Saul and his warriors would have enjoyed a great feast on the best parts of the "burnt offerings."

Samuel's reply to Saul is one of the clearest indications of what God desires: the sacrifice of self-will, rather than anything external.

And Samuel said, The Lord is not as well-pleased with burnt offerings and sacrifices as with one who obeys his voice. Behold, to obey is better than sacrifices, and to hearken, than the fat of rams. (1 Samuel 15:22)

Or as said in a reading:

For, He has given, no sacrifice is acceptable save as of the *desires* of self to be one with Him. (531-5)

Other Amalekites must have survived, for they are reported to have raided the town of Ziklag in David's absence. (1 Samuel 30) They weren't completely destroyed until the time of Hezekiah. (1 Chronicles 4:43)

"Music Hath Its Charms"

The mental unbalance taking place in Saul keeps revealing itself more and more distinctly as his reign continues. The most transparent example is with the "evil spirit" that began to possess him. The need to exorcise it brought David into Saul's life.

But the Spirit of the Lord departed from Saul, and an evil spirit from before the Lord troubled him.

And Saul's servants said to him, Behold, your servants are before you; Let them seek out a man who can play well on the harp; and when the evil spirit is upon you, he will play with his hands, and you shall be well. (1 Samuel 16:14–16)

Edgar Cayce talked of David's music.

"The evil spirit was perhaps nothing more than Saul's guilty conscience. After David's anointing, (1 Samuel 16:1–13) no doubt Saul—though knowing nothing of it consciously—became uneasy. He had a feeling something had gone wrong. In other words, he had the 'blues'! And David's playing chased them away. It made him forget he was out of tune.

"Even then Saul could have repented. But, as so many of us do today, he hardened his heart. We seek outside things to chase our 'blues' away, when what we need to do is to keep them from coming. We can do this by doing something constructive which will counteract those influences, or vibrations, around us which are the results of our own wrongdoing.

"Saul was so egotistical. The thing he was fighting was his own self and self-will. David's music brought back to Saul the consciousness of better things. Having once been aroused to the divine awareness within, one can, at some moments, easily approach the same awareness. The music quieted Saul's anger. In those moments, Saul was able to forget what he was losing."

We find this advice about music in one reading:

. . . whenever there are the periods of depression, or the feeling low or forsaken, play music; especially stringed instruments of every nature. These will enable [one] to span that gulf as between pessimism and optimism. (1804–1)

And Saul said to his servants, Provide me now a man who can play well, and bring him to me.

Then one of the young men answered and said, Behold I have seen a son of Jesse the Beth-lehemite, who is skillful in playing, a man of war and prudent in speech, a handsome man, and the Lord is with him.

Wherefore King Saul sent messengers to Jesse and said, Send me David your son; he will be useful to me. (1 Samuel 16:17–19)

These comments about mental unbalance and self-government are applicable to Saul.

Q–1. What relaxation [is] best for the body, in addition to that given?
A–1. Just that! Changing of the mental status is ever the builder, mental and physical. That as the mind dwells upon is builded. When one overtaxes one portion to the detriment of another, an *unbalancing* must ensue. Keep much in the manner as has been given, as regarding diet, exercise, work, perseverance. *Be* consistent in all thou doest, and when thou hast conquered self thou mayest be able to govern another. He who approaches for mercy, grace, and counsel may not have aught against his brother, but must be

able to appreciate and understand that he already has in hand. (257-53)

The Giant Killer

David's first residence at the court of Saul was only temporary. He returned to Bethlehem and tended his sheep. Possibly ten or fifteen years passed between his first summons to play for the king and the battle with Goliath.

"When David was anointed, apparently he had no idea he would be king someday. He felt he had been anointed for some special task he was to perform for King Saul.

"For years the Israelites had been fighting off the Philistines, and now they were about to give up. All the army felt none could defy Goliath. It was useless to try. They were about to give up. Then, because he had the right purpose and knew God was with him, David put an end to the war with one shot from his sling. This shows us what power there is in the smallest and most insignificant weapon, if our purpose is set in the Lord."

Two Souls Knit

After his victory over Goliath, David was summoned by Saul to recount the battle for him. David described his victory for the court, and when he finished, one of the most remarkable and memorable events of the Old Testament followed.

When David had finished speaking to Saul, the soul of Jonathan was knit to the soul of David, and Jonathan loved him as his own soul. (1 Samuel 18:1)

The Edgar Cayce readings demonstrate time and time again that our response and reactions to many individuals stem from "karmic memories." These "memories" are stored in the subconscious mind as emotional patterns which have been created by past associations in former lives. When old friends, lovers, enemies, or comrades encounter each other anew, the "memories" are released as spontaneous emotions.

Similarly, the subconscious responds when "like confronts like." People who hold certain values and ideals find themselves drawn to their own mental and spiritual kind.

In Life Reading 4219 an incarnation as Jonathan was given. Cayce described the earliest experience of the soul at the time of Genesis 1, ". . . when the forces showed the Sons coming together for the Glory of the earth's plane." (4219–3) *

Familiarity with this first experience of Jonathan's inspired this unique interpretation for the Bible class:

"It is very unusual to find the expression that the soul of Jonathan was 'knit' to the soul of David. No doubt their souls had been knit in purpose from the very beginning, or from the time of the creation of souls.

"This would account for their instant kinship."

A Disdain for Intrigue

Mr. 221, who in his life reading was told he had been King Saul, was described as being "subtle in the ultra-extent of carrying out purposes, good and bad." This trait is in evidence in Saul, and Edgar Cayce charted its course.

Saul's first reactions to David, like Jonathan's, were also favorable.

"Like Jonathan, Saul was also 'taken' with David after his victory with Goliath. David had become a great hero in one day, and the least Saul could do was to recognize what he had done and show appreciation for it. It wasn't until later that Saul realized David was

*See *A Million Years to the Promised Land: Edgar Cayce's Story of the Old Testament.*

going to replace him. He knew it long before David even suspected it.

"When all the people, including the king's own servants, began to honor David, and the women sang his praises, Saul became very jealous. We seldom feel this emotion unless we feel some lack within ourselves. Perhaps Saul was jealous because he knew David was more deserving of praise than he. When we are sure of ourselves there is no cause for jealousy.

"Saul's jealousy preyed upon him, and he began to plot against David's life. If a small canker is not discouraged, it can grow until it becomes ungovernable and takes possession of the whole being.

"Saul was the best spearsman in Israel. He could cast a spear within a hair's breadth of any target. Yet he was not able to kill David. According to his own interpretation, the Lord had deflected his hand. Whenever Saul came to himself, he was sorry he had sought David's life. But soon afterwards his jealousies were rekindled.

"When Saul failed the first time, his next emotion was fear. In order to feel secure, he began to placate David, and offered him his eldest daughter, Merab, in marriage. This was a tremendous move on Saul's part. Judging by David's reaction, we could only say he did not think himself suitable (socially) to be the king's son-in-law. It just did not make sense. David's reaction must have made Saul feel powerful again. He gave Merab in marriage to Adriel, the Meholathite.

"When Saul discovered Michal was in love with David, it pleased him. This was another opportunity to undo David. Saul was very sly this time. He used his soldiers, and let them persuade David that the slaying of a hundred Philistines would make him worthy of being a king's son-in-law. David must have loved Michal. It wasn't hard to convince him. He went out and killed TWO hundred, twice the number required. Saul had been sure David would be killed. Having made this stipulation, Saul was forced to give Michal to David.

"Instead of helping Saul with his plans, Michal was in love with David and ready to defend him. David now the king's son-in-law, was in social rank a prince, and was ever more a threat to Saul—or so Saul felt—and he became more and more afraid."

Approximately a year after the life readings for Saul and Jonathan, a young traveling salesman, a resident of a small town near Dayton, requested a life reading.

It was given on February 26, 1925. In it, the young man was told he had been Jonathan's armor bearer.

The armor bearer figures in only one episode in the Old Testament, that of the remarkable victory over the Philistine garrison at Michmash. (1 Samuel 14:6–15) No personal features are given about the armor bearer in this account. Indeed, not even his name is recorded. Yet Cayce's description of the entity helps to build an intuitive picture about the nature and character of this anonymous Biblical character.

Whereas Saul was "subtle in the ultraextent" in carrying out his purposes, we find in this entity a disdain for intrigue and underhanded techniques. Possibly this could have resulted from a life-time of first hand experiences in the court of Saul.

After the suggestion by the conductor of the reading, Edgar Cayce began:

Yes, we have the entity and its reaction in the present sphere with the Universal Forces as are exhibited in the physical body in the present earth's plane . . . we have in this body . . . the influences that make a very remarkable personage in the present plane, for we have one that truth, the ennobling influences, that are latent in every act of the entity. One also that the truth is paramount with the entity. One that the love of home and of connections are always in the actions of the body, yet there enters some of the adverse conditions through these [astrological aspects] . . . One who will give much influence in the rule to others, when guided, guarded, and directed in the proper channel.

One sensitive of nature, yet noble in thought and act. One timid in manner, yet one capable of reaching heights in expressing that in which the body is well founded in and believes the truth of.

One that has little to do with intrigue and underhand operations. One that thinks less of self should [he] allow [himself] to be misled, or drawn into such intrigues. Hence the purpose must ever be that never of self-condemnation, but rather relying on those elements that would make the sure and the paramount issue of life. Then one that should not place too much confidence in others. While this is not of a fault, yet the nature of this entity finding there was fault loses faith in self. Hence the greater forces should be exercised in placing that faith, that confidence, that purpose, in Him, the Giver of All Good and Perfect Gifts. (2888-2)

Cayce foresaw a brilliant career in real estate if the entity would renew his contact with the person he had known as Jonathan, who was now a land broker in nearby Dayton.

As to the abilities of the entity in the present earth's plane, with the ennobling influences, with the forces as lead the higher elements as an exhibition of the forces manifest, these should be, and would be, made a success in following that of real estate salesman, and this may be accomplished through some with whom this entity once was associated in times past, as we shall see. (2888-2)

Cayce then described 2888's most recent past life, as the secretary to Lord Baltimore in Maryland. Then, in the preceding incarnation:

. . . we find in the days when the rebellion was in the hand of the king, the first king, in Israel, and we find the entity then the armor bearer to Jonathan and in the present plane we find this personality: That of the innate desire to defend that which is a principle in the mind and heart of the body. In this relation we would find these experiences which would develop this entity in present earth plane would be under the influence of him who represented that entity then, for [he] is in this sphere at present. (2888-2)

Cayce then described an Arabian incarnation in which the entity learned the worth of land and property, and ended with a recommendation.

Hence the abilities to compile these two forces [to advise and estimate], and with that of Jonathan's bring about the success in the real estate forces of today. (2888-2)

Concluding the reading, Cayce gave this counsel:

Then, to use and apply this as given, keep first the faith in Him, the Giver of All Good and Perfect Gifts, knowing that the physical body is the temple of the living God, and present same holy and acceptable unto Him, which is but a reasonable service, for in service to man the greater service is offered to God.
We are through. (2888-2)

In Pursuit of David

As a psychic, Edgar Cayce was never able to recall a word he spoke in trance. And while in trance, he responded only to the questions which were asked him, often by strangers concerned only with their bodily ills.
But the Tuesday night Bible class gave Edgar Cayce the opportunity to speak freely, philosophize, interpret, and expound upon the thing he knew and loved best— his Bible. As a young lad, Cayce had been drawn to the Book, and its mystery and fascination never diminished for him. He was able to take the Bible, and all

the aspects of life it contained, and interpret them on the basis of his own life experiences. And many and varied were the psychic and spiritual experiences in his life which he could draw upon.

But nowhere in the class are two characters more delineated than David and Saul. And nowhere in the Bible class does the story come closest to a dramatic narrative than when Edgar Cayce tells the story of Saul's pursuit of David.

The story begins with 1 Samuel 19 and continues through to the death of Saul.

Saul has already tried to impale David once with his javelin, and failed, and plotted unsuccessfully to have him killed in battle. David has become the king's son-in-law, and a soul-brother to Jonathan, and, due to his succession of victories over the Philistines, has been growing increasingly popular with the people.

Thus, the "evil spirit" vexed Saul, and he issued a proclamation.

And Saul told Jonathan his son and all his servants that they should kill David. (1 Samuel 19:1)

Cayce discussed the relationship between father and son.

"When Saul began plotting against David, Jonathan, as the prince, felt he could influence his father against his plans. Having once been anointed, and having experienced the spirit of the Lord, Saul could, occasionally, be appealed to. Jonathan appealed to the good in Saul, reminding him of all the wonderful things David had done for him and his kingdom. Temporarily Saul tried to live up to the best within himself. He knew deep within that he was at fault, not David. But Saul was wishy-washy. His own selfish desires got the best of him.

"He openly proclaimed that he sought David's life. This caused great consternation to the people who loved David, yet felt they must follow their king. Perhaps the people, at this point, began to regret that they had demanded a king."

David fled to Ramtha, and Saul followed. At Ramtha, Saul encountered Samuel with a company of prophets. Face-to-face with the venerable sage, Saul abandoned the chase, stripped off his clothes, and prophesied.

Although Saul began his reign with the reputation as a prophet, there was a lack of sincerity in this experience which Edgar Cayce detected.

"Everyone who came into Samuel's presence began to prophesy. No wonder the people began to question themselves whether Saul was really a prophet, or to be considered one any longer."

Neither David nor Jonathan understood why Saul was so intent upon David's life. Neither of the men knew of any offense or crime of which David was guilty.

The following day was the feast of the new moon, a holiday banquet for Saul's warriors and dignitaries. David knew he would be missed and that Saul would ask about him. David decided to use this situation to test the temper of the king. Jonathan agreed to his part in the plan, a simple ruse through which David could have his worst suspicions confirmed or allayed.

For Edgar Cayce, it was a lesson on "to tell the truth."

"We find many instances where David saved his life by evading the truth. It shows his cautiousness. He treated poison with poison. Saul, knowing David was anxious to return to his own people, had forbidden it. David, then, used this to mislead Saul. Perhaps the purpose justified his actions. Some people feel it is best to *always* tell the truth, regardless of the consequences.

"We do know if we say or do anything against our higher self, or our own conscience, it is wrong. In this instance, David's lie hurt no one. What is wrong for one person can be right for another, depending upon the purpose behind the act."

"Jonathan agreed to David's plan. He didn't really believe Saul would kill David."

Because Saul became enraged when he heard he had gone home to offer the traditional yearly sacrifice with his family, David knew his life was in jeopardy. David fled, beginning his life as a fugitive from Saul.

His first stop was in Noh, at the house of Ahimeleck, a priest. This time David practiced another deception, but with disastrous results for the priest and his family.

Then David came to Noh, to Ahimeleck the priest; and Ahimeleck was afraid at meeting David, and said to him, Why have you come alone, and no man with you? (1 Samuel 21:1)

"Ahimeleck had every reason to be afraid. News of Saul's anger had spread throughout the country. Saul had published several edicts against David. But David misrepresented himself. He said the king had sent him, which was the truth in one sense, since he was fleeing from Saul. But he gave the impression to Ahimeleck that Saul had sent him on a mission of importance. The priest didn't know whether David was there on business or not.

"According to the custom, the bread of the tabernacle, which David asked for, should have been destroyed. No one was supposed to have it. Because there was nothing else to give him strength, David persuaded the priest to give him the hallowed bread —not just enough for himself, but for the many men whom the priest assumed were with David.

"We see how powerful Saul and David had become. The priests listened to them rather than standing firm in the laws of God in which they had been trained.

"Later Ahimeleck and all his household were killed for just this conversation with David."

David's next encounter was with Achish, king of Gath.

And David arose and fled that day from fear of Saul, and went to Achish the king of Gath. (1 Samuel 21:10)

Edgar Cayce detected elements of David's statesmanship in this episode.

"The servants of Achish had heard the songs praising David. They thought he was actually the king of the Israelites. Consequently they questioned his unprecedented appearance among them. Then David pretended he was insane. He knew they would let him go if they thought he had lost his reason. He would be of no consequence to them.

"David was quite a diplomat!"

While Saul moved in on the house of Ahimeleck and massacred its inhabitants, David fled into the wild country of Arlam. There he was joined by every man who was in distress, in debt, or discontented, about four hundred in all.

Only one priest of eighty-five survived the slaughter Saul had ordered for Ahimeleck. Abiathar, Ahimeleck's grandson, escaped and joined David. When David heard about the massacre, he took the blame on himself. He realized the whole tragedy could have been avoided if he had not been so overconfident. He didn't try to excuse himself, but accepted the fault as his. He promised Abiathar protection.

Although David was a fugitive, he retained his loyalty to Saul and Israel. Whenever a threat or danger was posed to an Israelite town or settlement, David and his men went to its rescue.

Edgar Cayce called David "the original Robin Hood."

Then they told David, saying, Behold, the Philistines are fighting against Keilah and are robbing the

*threshing floors. And David inquired of the Lord, say-
ing, Shall I go and smite the Philistines and save
Keilah? And the Lord said to him, Go and smite the
Philistines and save Keilah. (1 Samuel 23:1–2)*

Cayce asked:

"In what way did David communicate with the Lord?
Abiathar was a priest who used the ephod to enquire.
Or David may have received his own answer from
the voice within. All the Israelites knew the body was
the temple, and that God had promised to meet everyone in his own temple. If we inquire, if we enter
within, the answer comes. Moses' last admonition to
the people had been that they be guided by the still
small voice within.

"Perhaps the answer came to David as a voice, in
a vision, or just a 'feeling.' The main thing to realize
is that David inquired and received an answer.

"When his people appeared doubtful, David inquired again, just to be sure he was right in marching against the Philistines. Two hundred more of the
men of Judah joined him in the fight, and they saved
Keilah. Yet there were those among them who would
turn David over to Saul if the right opportunity arose.
David discovered this by inquiring through the ephod.
He and his men then fled into the wilderness."

For a man seeking information about buried treasure
through a psychic reading, Edgar Cayce pointed him to
the same source which David and other seekers obtained their guidance.

Q-1. Will it be the proper time to go now?
A-1. As has been given, such decisions are to be directed by that within self that answers to the influences or forces from without—but the answers and
directions must come from within; rather than by any
helping hand.

Rememberest thou all that has been given as to the manner in which the individual finds self? Did Moses receive direction save by the period in the mount? Did Samuel receive rather than by meditating within his own closet? Did David not find more in the meditating within the valley and the cave? Did not the Master in the mount and in the Garden receive the answers of those directing forces?

These as directions, these as omens, these as signs ONLY, and the direction from the inward closer walk with thine inner self and thy purposes and thy desire. (707–6)

Saul and David are a study in contrasts, and nowhere is the difference more clearly emphasized than in what each felt God had called them to do.

When Saul was advised of David's victory at Keilah, and that David was still in the city, Saul felt, because he had an opportunity to kill David, that God was on his side again.

. . . and Saul said, God has delivered him into my hands; for he has shut himself up by entering a town that has gates and bars. (1 Samuel 23:7)

Time and again, in his persecution of him, David had the opportunity to destroy Saul. But he wouldn't do it. He felt that the Lord had something more special for him to do than to kill the king and take his place.

Advised that he had been betrayed by citizens of Keilah who were sympathetic to Saul, David and his men took refuge in the wilderness forests of Ziph. There they were visited by Jonathan.

"Jonathan came to David in the forest, and strengthened him in his faith. This was the first time David realized he was going to be the king. Jonathan told him he would be, and that he, Jonathan, would be next to him in power, and that Saul knew all this.

"Jonathan knew David was God's chosen vessel. He knew it by the way David conducted himself, and by the way the people loved him.

"David escaped to the wilderness of Ziph, and the Ziphites took advantage of the situation to gain favor with Saul. Just as Saul was closing in, a messenger arrived with news of an invasion of Philistines. The Philistines knew a house divided could not stand, and they were working hard to establish a stronghold in Israel.

"We wonder if the message, which allowed David to get away, had been sent by Jonathan."

After pursuing the Philistines, Saul resumed his hunt for David. However, this time God delivered Saul into David's hands.

. . . and Saul went into the cave and lay down there; and David and his men were staying on the slope of the cave. And the men of David said to him, Behold, this is the day of which the Lord said to you, Behold, I will deliver your enemy into your hands, that you may do to him as shall seem good in your sight. Then David arose and cut off the skirt of Saul's robe stealthily. (1 Samuel 24:3–4)

Once David cut Saul's skirt, he felt it was wrong. He called to the king from a high hill and begged his forgiveness.

"David could never get over the fact that Saul was God's anointed. He regretted cutting the skirt, and made obeisance to Saul. For the first time, he asked his forgiveness.

"Saul melted in the face of David's humility. You see, Saul KNEW what was right. He recognized the godliness David presented to him through his humility. But Saul was unstable. When he was left alone, his jealousies and fears overtook him.

"Aren't we like Saul? We can be swayed emotionally at times, and vow to make great sacrifices and do big things. But when it comes right down to our daily life, we fall back into old habits and think first and foremost of our own desires.

"Notice Saul exacted a promise from David, which he kept. Saul did not keep his."

The exchange of promises gave David a brief respite from the chase. In the intervening time, until Saul again renewed his relentless pursuit, Samuel died (25:1) and David met and married Abigail, the rich young widow whose husband David had been ready to slay for personal reasons. (25:2–44)

Cayce felt Nabal had pricked David's ego by not giving him the same recognition he was used to receiving from everyone else.

"After Abigail came to him, David began to realize what he had almost done. He was going to slay Nabal and all his house because of personal anger. It had not ever occurred to him to inquire of the Lord first. He realized what a great sin would have been his if Abigail hadn't come to him first.

"She was very smart, no doubt already in love with David, or, at least a great admirer. When she returned home she must have told Nabal what she had done in such a way that, with his physical condition weakened from over-indulgence, it produced heart failure."

Following this interlude, the Ziphites again informed Saul about David's location. Saul returned to the wilderness of Giboath once more, and while Saul slept, David had his second opportunity to slay the king.*

*Because of their many similarities, many commentors feel the two episodes of chapters 24 and 26 are the same event. Yet Edgar Cayce felt differently. He based his opinion on the fact that David sent spies out to confirm the rumors that Saul had renewed the chase (26:4), indicating he did not at first believe Saul had broken his promises and come out against him.

*So David and Abishai came to the people by night;
and behold, Saul lay asleep in the path, with his spear
lying on the ground . . . Then said Abishai to David,
Your God had delivered your enemy into your hands
this day; now therefore let me smite him just once
with this spear which is on the ground, and I will not
smite him the second time. (1 Samuel 26:7–8)*

This episode occasioned a philosophical reflection by
Edgar Cayce on the subject of attitudes toward tyrants.

"Abishai wanted to kill Saul. He felt it was too good
an opportunity to pass by. Yet David wanted to
protect the king. He still respected Saul as God's
Anointed.

"There is a fine line of distinction drawn here. Considering that none are in authority save by the power
of God, just what should our attitude toward tyrants
and dictators be today who, so far as we can see,
have no fear of God inside them. We can always turn
to the example of Jesus. The Romans in his day were
attempting to overrun the world and enslave all the
conquered nations. Did Jesus raise an army and stand
up to his oppressors. He could have done so, and won.
Yet he showed a better way.

"David was aware of this same spiritual law. He
said to Abishai, 'As the Lord liveth, the Lord shall
smite him; or he shall descend in battle and perish.'
The wicked will perish by their own hands. Or, if you
give them enough rope, they'll hang themselves. Saul
eventually died on his own sword.

"Let us remember, it is only justifiable to destroy
life when the whole intent and purpose of that life
is to do evil. Saul had many good qualities. Many
times he repented and, for short periods, tried to overcome his own personal ambition and jealousies.

"Today, when we look at leaders who are responsible for so much suffering, we sometimes feel that their
destruction would be a blessing for mankind. Yet who
are we to judge? The leaders are not solely responsible.

If there had not been the need and desire by the majority, that leader could not have risen to power. But there must come a purging. Those who live by the sword, die by the sword. Those who trust only in the strength of their weapons, must one day be overcome by their own wrong actions.

"As David indicated, time will tell. We must not allow our hearts to be filled with hatred for those who are attempting to rule by force. We should make every effort at keeping humble, in readiness to be directed by His will. Remember, there is no such thing as a coincidence. There is a reason for everything that happens to us, around us, and in this world."

After this episode, David re-entered the territory of Gath. He wanted to escape to a land where Saul had no jurisdiction. In Gath, he would no longer be considered a threat by Saul.

But time had run out for Saul. Samuel was dead. David was still popular. The Philistine armies were amassing for another battle.

In this last battle, Jonathan was slain and Saul died on his own sword. David had been tried and tested, and had proven himself equal to Samuel's expectation—"a man after God's heart."

Saul and the Witch of Endor
Spirit Communication

Saul knew for some time that he had marked out a dark future for himself of death and defeat. Yet, like all men, he hoped this destruction could be avoided. After the death of Samuel, there was no longer a prophet in Israel. Like Saul, many of the Israelites had abandoned their traditional religion. Many worshipped pagan deities. There was no longer anyone to whom Saul could turn.

And when Saul inquired of the Lord, he did not answer him, either by dreams or by fire or by prophets. Then Saul said to his servants, Seek me a woman

*who has a familiar spirit, that I may go to her and
inquire of her. And his servants said to him, Behold,
there is a woman who has a familiar spirit at En-dor.
(1 Samuel 28:7)*

Edgar Cayce drew a distinction between "diviners"
in the Bible and those who had familiar spirits. A "divin-
er" was one who sought to be directed by the spirit of
Truth; in the highest sense, one who continuously sought
to do God's Will. One with a "familiar spirit" was a
medium who allowed himself to be possessed by departed entities who were themselves still in a state of
development (or regression).

Throughout the Old Testament, mediumship was never
commended. It was prohibited by Mosaic Law, and later
condemned by the prophets. Throughout their history,
Israel was always directed in its seeking to go to the
highest source, the spirit of God which could be found
within.

Saul, who began his reign with a spiritual awakening,
seldom followed the promptings of the Spirit. He who
never heeded Samuel when the prophet was alive, troubled him for advice after he had died.

*And Saul disguised himself and put on other rai-
ment, and he went to the woman by night; and Saul
said to her, Divine for me by the familiar spirit, and
bring up for me him whom I shall tell you.*

*Then the woman said, Whom shall I bring up to
you? And he said, Bring me up Samuel ...*

*And the woman said to Saul, I saw gods ascending
out of the earth ... And she said to him, An old man
is coming up; and he is covered with a mantle. And
Saul perceived that it was Samuel ...*

*And Samuel said to Saul, Why have you disturbed
me to bring me up? (1 Samuel 28:8–16)*

The Cayce readings show how closely connected the
unseen and seen worlds are. Spirit communication is an

authentic phenomena, yet it was warned against and never recommended as something to be sought after.

Q–12. . . . is it possible for an ego itself either receding through what we call inter-stellar space, or existing on another [plane of consciousness] to so keep in touch, or so be aware of little finite details on the earth plane, as to guide in detail . . . one whom that ego may choose to guide?
A–12. That is correct; this is possible, but the care must be taken by such an one that they be guided in that contact from one receding through stellar space, by the same desire as is made manifest by one so receding and seeking to aid . . . for when one is misdirected, we may find such an example in the seeking of the king to be guided by him, who annoyed him while the desire called up the old man, and the answer: "Why disturbest thou me, know [ye] not there has already been created the lasciviousness of desire earthly, in the actitivites, that destruction is already before thee." Study that, see? (136–83)

A warning was given to a group who desired to experiment with and record psychic forces.

. . . those who accredit or seek or desire other sources . . . the more oft they will be found to be such as those that are patterns or examples in Holy Writ; namely an excellent one—Saul, the first king. Here we find an example of an individual seeking from the man of God, or the prophet, information to be given clairvoyantly, telepathically (if you choose to use such terms); and we find the incident used as an illustration that may be well kept to the forefront in the minds of those who would prompt or check or record such experiments. (792–2)

There are many ordinances regarding mediumship throughout the Bible. Spirit communication and mediumship were topics under frequent discussion in the Bible class. When the class reached the point in their study where Saul, in his desperation, turned to the witch of Endor, Cayce used the opportunity to present his views on spirit communication.

"Many people feel that when a soul passes from the earth, it becomes all-wise and can counsel those who are still here. But, as the tree falls, so does it lie. Samuel did not have any greater power nor any greater wisdom because he had passed over. He rebuked Saul, and repeated what he had already told him.

" 'Why has thou disquieted me, to bring me up?'

"This rebuke from Samuel should be the answer for us today. When a soul leaves this earth plane, it has work to do in other realms of consciousness. Unless it is an earthbound soul—and certainly we do not wish to seek guidance from an earthbound entity—it is finished with the cares of this world for the present.

"Our answer should be—it is not right to seek communication with departed entities.

"If we seek to be guided by the Christ, we can accept the messenger He sends, whether it be in the form of a loved one, an angel, or a stranger. Saul had not heeded Samuel's counsel when he was alive. How could he expect Samuel to advise him differently, just because he had passed from the earth plane?

"When Jesus was transfigured on the mount, Moses and Elijah materialized at his side, and talked with him about the things that were to happen. This experience was a natural consequence of His attunement with God, and came as an assurance.

"We may all have similar experiences if we seek first the kingdom of God. But we should never go out of our way to seek it through familiar spirits."

Several years earlier, the philosophy in this lecture was first expressed in reading.

Then, how may one determine in one's own experience as to the value or the reliability of information that may be given through any channel that may propose to be, or that may be said to be, of a psychic nature ...

"Try ye the spirits," ye have been admonished; and they that testify that He has *come*, that bespeak such in their activities, are of TRUTH.

Then, they that bring to each soul—not comfort, not as earthly pleasure, but—that which is *spiritually constructive in the experience of a soul, are worthy of acceptance* ...

What sought Saul? For his own satisfying of his conscience, or for the edification of that which might bring truth? Because the soul of Samuel had entered into that inter-between did not change one iota the position that Saul bore with constructive influences. While the *channel* might be questioned, the souce— and that received—was truth! For it came from the source that had already warned Saul. (5752-5)

Chapter 7

King David

Abner

With Saul's death, there was nothing to hinder David's rise to power. He had always been popular with the people. Now he was certain to gain ever more popularity, influence and power.

> *Now there was a long war between the house of Saul and the house of David, but David grew stronger, and the house of Saul became weaker and impoverished. (2 Samuel 3:1)*

The Bible records an incident which seems a decisive factor in ending the war. Abner, Saul's general, remained loyal to Ashbashul, Saul's son, and supported him as king over the tribes of Israel, while David ruled over the tribe of Judah.

After two years of Ashbashul's reign, Abner changed his loyalties.

> *And Saul had a concubine whose name was Rizpah, the daughter of Ana; and Ashbashul said to Abner, Why are you going in unto my father's concubine?*
>
> *Then Abner was exeeedingly displeased at the word of Ashbashul, and Abner said, . . . I show kindness to the house of Saul . . . and have not delivered you*

into the hand of David, and yet you charge me with iniquity concerning a woman. So do God and more to Abner, if I do not perform what the Lord has spoken to David, even so will I do, to transfer the kingdom from the house of Saul, and to establish the throne of David over Israel and over Israel from Dan to Beersheba.

And Ashbashul could not reply to Abner, because he feared him. (2 Samuel 3:7–11)

Cayce philosophized on the significance of this episode.

"What a little thing it takes to change the whole course of a man's life, or even a nation's. Ashbashul's faultfinding changed the whole course of the Israelite tribes. It aroused Abner to action. There had been a lull between the Philistines and the Israelites, and Abner was having a quiet time.

"He determined to translate all his energies into helping David become king. Abner knew about the prophecies concerning David. He probably felt it was going to happen anyway, and he might as well have a hand in making it possible.

"Abner still had great influence over the people, and he used it to urge them to accept David as king. He knew David could have made himself king, even before Saul's death, and that he hadn't chosen to do it."

On February 8, 1939, a life reading was given for a teen-age Protestant boy. In the opening preamble, he was described as "a natural leader, a natural politician, making for, then, even in little details, the activities in which the purposes and intents will be carried out." The parents were also warned their son was "very susceptible to the fair sex."

Then, an incarnation as Abner was described.

... the entity was among those who were close to the king who was proclaimed after Saul—or a friend of, a companion of David; and raised to one in power—yet the experience became both an advancement as well as a retardment. For the entity allowed self, and the power of self, to become as the greater influence.

The name then was Abner.

Yet as for power, as for influence, as for the musical forces, as for the thrusts, as for the directing powers and forces among men, this is a great force and influence in the present experience.

Hence again, God and right, God and faithfulness, God and truth is to be the motto of the entity in all of its relationships.

Hence the spiritual side of the nature of the entity is to be impressed and directed. And have no instructor, no director that is not well grounded in SPIRITUAL things! (1815-2)

The life reading laid the foundation for Cayce's final assessment of this significant figure in Israel's history.

"Would Abner be called a good man? Perhaps Abner could be described as a good military leader, and a good moral man; though he never quite understood what it meant—as David did—to rely entirely upon the Lord."

"A Man After God's Heart

The instability of Saul's relationship to God is a fine contrast to the sturdiness which David shows in his. The stature of David is measured in several ways in the readings. He was described as an example for man as a man, and yet the readings also reach out and touch upon his metaphysical and cosmic significance.

We find him among those who contributed to the development of the Christ.

For without Abraham, without Moses, yea without David, what need could there be that Melchizedek, that Enoch, or Joseph, or Joshua, should again come in the flesh? fulfilling all?

Have ye fulfilled all? When ye have, ye are One with Him ... (1158–9)

David's name is the only one included in Cayce's list of those who developed the God-relationship which is not an incarnation of the soul Jesus.

... activity toward the proper understanding and proper relationships to that which is the making for the closer relationships to that which is in Him *alone*. Ye have seen it in Adam; ye have heard it in Enoch, ye have had it made known in Melchizedek; Joshua, Joseph, David, and those that made the preparation then for him called Jesus. (5749–5)

The significance of David's name is measured by its meaning. All who are named David share in its vibration. Cayce chose to call a friend by his middle rather than given name.

Q–3. Why is this body so often referred to as David, rather than Edwin David, in psychic readings as given by Edgar Cayce?
A–3. The development of the entity is rather in that vibration of David than of Edwin, for these two conditions are with the vibration in the names; Edwin, meaning that of a peacefulness, defender of peacefulness, carrying both the condition and implied forces from same. David, rather that of the gift from the higher forces, or a Son of the Father. One, especially, endowed with gifts from higher forces. (137–13)

As a model for man, and as one that was to set an ideal, King David made full use of his talents. He was a well-rounded personality, versatile and gifted, who could claim equal fame as a soldier, statesman, poet, composer, and musician. And yet, as this reading indicates, he is an example of humility.

Who, having named the name of the Christ, has become conscious of that He represented or presented in the world? As the records have been handed down that Abraham represents the faithful, Moses meekness, David the warrior yet humility, so the Christ represents Love; that all may know that He hath paid the price for all. (262-56)

As an example for man, one of David's greatest attributes is in his ability to celebrate. When he was sorrowful, he prayed; but when he was joyful, he danced and sang and played, giving praise and thanksgiving for the glories of God.

Throughout his life he remained keenly aware of Nature. He was attuned to the beauties in all forms and walks of Life. He was able to see God manifesting in everything!

Then, play as well as work. Relax as well as keep taut. So, through the mental abilities of the body, be as appreciative of the finer things of life as of material success. Be as capable of appreciating the beggar with a God-given voice as would bring tears of appreciation of love of man for man or woman, or of the appreciation of the beauties in nature, as appreciative of the man with a million, able to wield a power and influence of a nature that shows and belies of self-aggrandizement of power. Be, through the mental abilities, so as to be appreciative of that in art, or beauty in a picture, or beauty in nature. Let these, as they did to thine own peoples—even thine prophet, thine servant David, as he declared in, "The glory of God is made manifest! Even the heavens declare His glory and the firmament showeth His handiwork"; for fame and fortune often take wings and fly away—but one appreciative of the beauties in nature, in the abilities of His handmaid, in the might of Him that serves in song or dance, or the piper, these also declare His glory—and, as these be appreciated, so may that as may be given in this world's goods, in power, in might, in moneys, in position—so one may know how, through what channel, one may serve . . . These are but little things in the eyes of many. These, by their very foolishness to many, confound the wise. These but make contentment that makes one seek and seek for knowledge of Him that gives the gifts *in* life; for He be the God of the *living* whom thou servest, and material things are but dead—and are dead *weight* when one has not attuned self to the beauties in every field that makes manifest.

Even the toad is as beautiful in the sight of the Creator as the lily, and he that heedeth not the little things may not be master of the great things, for he that was capable of using the talents in the little way was made the ruler over *great* cities.

Keep thine body fit. Keep thine mind attuned to beauty. (257-53)

Because David was faithful with the little things, he was able to handle the great matters. Rabbinical traditions state, as a shepherd, David treated his sheep tenderly, with loving care. Therefore God said, "He understands how to pasture sheep; therefore he shall become shepherd of my flock, Israel."

Although David grew in his ability to master all aspects of life, there were many times he was not able to conquer the desire to sin. He was tempted in many ways and succumbed often.

One of David's most remarkable gifts was his ability to take criticism. When Saul sinned and Samuel admonished him, Saul hardened his heart; whereas when Nathan rebuked David, David listened. When he was in error, David acknowledged it and blamed no one else for his shortcomings.

In June, 1937, David was cited as an example worthy of study for A.R.E. members assembled at their sixth annual congress.

Using the experience of David the king as an example, what was it in his experience that caused him to be called a man after God's own heart? That he did not falter? that he did not do this or that or be guilty of every immoral experience in the category of man's relationship? Rather was it that he was sorry, and not guilty of the same offense twice!

Well that ye pattern thy study of thyself after such a life! (5753-2)

The Pattern of a Life

Although there is little said in the readings about the life of David, in the Bible class Edgar Cayce dwelt on it at length and in detail. Saul and David were a study in contrasts, and Cayce drew many lessons from their variations. Saul is an example of a man at war within himself, unwilling to submit to the Spirit which had awakened him. This led to madness, self-destruction, and the termination of his house.

David's life witnesses to a remarkable spiritual growth throughout.

Edgar Cayce identified with both Saul and David, for he presented the two men in a believable, compassionate, and understanding way. Yet Cayce identified closely with David, as if he found in the king a model for his own life: a man who knew both weakness and strength, gifted in unusual ways and destined to fulfill a peculiar service.

Edgar Cayce's lectures on David reveal remarkable gems of insight and spiritual understanding which reveal a very unusual character—but whether the person is David or Edgar Cayce, the reader will have to decide.

Although the lectures are valuable, perhaps this reading gives us the key to the greatest similarity between Edgar Cayce and King David.

Study as to why David is called "a man—man—after God's own heart." Not that he was free from fault, but that his purposes, his hopes, his fears were continually submitted to God. And remember, as he

gave, "That which I feared has come upon me."
(4047–2)

The King

*And David perceived that the Lord had established
him king over Israel, and that he had exalted his kingdom for the sake of his people. (2 Samuel 5:12)*

David was crowned king at a unique time in world
history. The stage was set for the rise of Israel, and
David took full measure of the opportunity which was
given him.

In the southwest, the Egyptian empire was in decline.
In the east, the Assyrian and Babylonian empires which,
centuries later, would take Israel into bondage had not
yet arisen. On the highway between these two world
centers sat the new kingdom of Israel. In a few short
years David led the development of an insignificant nation into the single most powerful kingdom in the earth
at that time.

David was twenty-three when he was crowned king
over Judah, and thirty years old when he was made king
over the twelve tribes.

David's first act as king was to make the home of
Melchizedek, priest of the Most High, his capital. Jerusalem was among the cities which had remained unconquered by Joshua. It was an impregnable fortress, the
stronghold of the Jebusites. It was a strategic city, cen-
trally located on the trade-routes of the world.

After establishing "the city of God" as his capital,
David's next act was to bring the Ark of the Covenant
into the city.

Although there is an obvious military and political
significance to these acts, there is also a mystical, or
metaphysical meaning which supersedes. The strategy
which David followed to establish and unite his kingdom is similar to a pattern of spiritual understanding.

David, perhaps more than any king of Israel until Jesus,

understood the kingdom was first a spiritual one, which had to be built in the heart and mind of individuals before it could ever manifest outwardly. David, because he had done it within himself already, was able to bring the pattern of a heavenly kingdom into the earth.

Jerusalem—"the city of Melchizedek"—symbolizes a state of consciousness from which all men should rule, and make their capital, and return the Ark of the Covenant (knowledge of the laws) to it. Then, as David did after subduing all his enemies, we can begin planning for the Temple (which is the body).

The Death of Uzzah

The Ark of the Covenant had been abandoned, possibly for fifty or sixty years. Saul had never paid any attention to it, especially since his break with Samuel. And Samuel had not insisted that he should.

The Ark had not been in the tabernacle since the day Hophni and Phineas carried it into battle with the Philistines, and it was captured. (1 Samuel 4)

No doubt the tabernacle itself had gone into discard and deteriorated greatly, especially the outer coverings.

Following the conquest of Jerusalem, David chose twenty thousand men from all the tribes of Israel. He declared a national celebration and a great ceremonial procession, as they set out to return the Ark of the Covenant to the City of God.

However the great procession was marred by the death of Uzzah, an unexpected event which, in the countless generations that have followed, has caused men to speculate, ponder, and attempt to interpret its real significance.

And when they came to Nachon's threshingfloor, Uzzah put forth his hand to the ark of God, and took hold of it; for the oxen shook it. And the anger of the Lord was kindled against Uzzah; and God smote him for his error; and there he died by the ark of God. (2 Samuel 6:6–7)

Several traditions have grown out of the attempt to rationalize Uzzah's death. Why should a good man die for attempting to do a good deed? One rabbinical school holds that Uzzah was being punished for relieving himself too near the ark.

However, both the readings and the Bible class took note of this event, and supply insights into the happening.

Reading 440-16 describes Mount Sinai as being " . . . electrified by the presence of the God of the people and ohm of the Omnipotent to such an extent that no living thing could remain on same, save those two [Moses and Joshua] . . ." In Moses' time, the people still had a knowledge of electricity which probably had been handed down from Atlantis. In David's time, this knowledge was all but forgotten.

Research now indicates the Ark of the Covenant was a type of electric capacitor capable of producing an electrical charge of 500 to 700 volts. The Ark was made of acacia wood, lined inside and out with gold; or, two conductors separated by an insulator. The garlands on either side may have served as condensers. Insulated from the ground, the Ark is said to have given off fiery rays, acting like a Leyden jar. The capacitor was discharged to earth through the garlands. To move the Ark, two golden rods were slid through the rings attached to the exterior.*

In the Bible class, Edgar Cayce discussed the possibility of death by shock.

"The indication is that Uzzah only tried to steady the ark, to prevent it from falling. Apparently his purpose was good. There is no later reference to this except by Paul, who calls attention to the fact that one even in his lack of understanding suffered death. It could be that the vibrations were so high that they brought

*According to Maurice Denis-Papin, quoted in *Secrets of the Great Pyramid* by Peter Tompkins (New York: Harper & Row, 1971), p. 278.

death by shock, just as if he had touched a live electric wire.

"The ark had never been on a cart before the Philistines captured it. The priests always carried it on their shoulders. We might say our relationship to God is a personal thing. We can't put it on a new cart and have someone else haul it for us. Uzzah should have known better than to ever let it be put on the cart. If the oxen shook the ark, that in itself should have warned them it wasn't the right way."

While in the clairvoyant consciousness, Edgar Cayce drew on the illustration of Uzzah to answer the following question:

Q-2. Please explain the veil within the Holy of Holies.
A-2. . . . as that given by the Master, "These I have spoken in parable lest they see and are converted." What meaneth this?

That those individuals' times, purposes, intents, had not been completed or sufficient unto where they would be stable in their use or application of the glory or the opportunity or the factor itself.

So with the veil in the Holy of Holies, which might not be entered save by him who had been dedicated to the office of representing or presenting the purpose, the mind of the people as a whole—and *then* only after consecrating himself for that period or act of service . . . What brought death to him that put forth his hand to steady the Ark that, in *order*, sat behind the veil? That which had brought to that individual material prosperity, laudation among his brethren; yet the soul had accepted all without dedicating his body, his mind, his purpose to that service—breaking through the veil to accept and yet not showing forth that which was in keeping with those commands, those promises. For it had been said and given, "He that putteth forth his hand *beyond* that veil shall *surely* die!" (262–94)

Be not overanxious; for he that is overanxious,
even, is as Uzzah. (262-72)

Remember Er, Uzzah and Malchus?, how their cu-
riosity brought to them that period of night when that
they had builded must be accounted for. (262-72)

Bathsheba and the Sorrows of David

Perhaps one of David's greatest disappointments was
that he was forbidden to build the Temple of God. He
had been told by a prophet that he could not build the
Temple because he had "shed blood abundantly" and
waged great wars. (1 Chronicles 22:8) Although He
helped David completely subdue the Philistines, the
Moabites, Syrians, Ammonites, Amalekites, Edomites,
and all the other neighboring nations, God, in His wisdom
knew a man of war could not, or should not, build
His Temple.

If David built the Temple, there would be too much
bitterness among the defeated nations toward David's
God. In Solomon's generation much of the pain and hor-
ror of those wars had been healed and forgotten.

Perhaps another meaning might be read into this injunction. David, as a man who had waged war and
shed much blood, had no hesitation about instigating
the virtual murder of Uriah the Hittite in order to con-
ceal his own adultery with Bathsheba. His bloodletting
had hardened his heart to such an extent that he was
able, as one reading says, "to forget himself" and go to
a shocking extreme to get his own ends.

A young Hebrew woman, in her reading, was told
that following her incarnation as the daughter of Hur and
a helper to Moses and Aaron she had reincarnated at the
time of David.

> ... the entity was in the Holy Land, or the promised
> land; as the children of Judah gathered to proclaim
> their confidence, their faith in David the king, who
> worshipped God in a manner such that it was given,

"a man after mine own heart." Not that he failed not, but not guilty of the same offense twice, and gave credit ever to God—not to self; the GLORY to God, the weakness acknowledged in self, but the glory to Him.

There we find the entity was a handmaiden to Bathsheba, in those periods when she became the companion to David—under those periods of disturbance when there was the forgetting of self and Uriah was slain; when, as Nathan declared, "Thou art the man." [2 Samuel 12:7]

The entity then was that assistant or companion to the body guard of David, in the name Shelah. The entity gained from those experiences; LEARNED much from the sorrows of Bathsheba, as well as of David.

And in the present through the abilities to help others, who find great sorrow in their lives from incidents, accidents, or even from premeditated efforts to take advantage of situations, the entity may counsel with those of her own sex as well as those of the young, in preparing them for meeting the vicissitudes in life's highway.

In the experience the entity gained through the greater part of the sojourn. Well may the tenets of the 1st, the 24th, and the 90th Psalms become as a part of the entity's meditation, in seeking for that atonement with that ONLY which brings peace in self and in the experience or associations with others, as of an at-onement with that Creative Force or God. (2796–1)

It is not clear when in David's reign his adultery with Bathsheba took place. As a chronology the sequence of events in Scripture are not historical.* The promise

*That the Bible is accurate history in terms of chronology is a notion that dies hard. The Edgar Cayce readings, such as on Genesis, show the symbolic rather than literal nature of the narrative in which a day, a year, or an epoch can be covered in

to David of an eternal throne is recounted in chapter 7, and takes place at a time "when the king dwelt in his house and the Lord had given him rest from his enemies." Yet in chapter 11, which tells the story of Bathsheba, Israel was at war, besieging Rabbath, a strong Ammonite fortress.

We learn from reading 601–5 that it was not until after his marriage to Bathsheba that there were "favorable periods" for the spread of David's influence over his people and the neighboring nations. Therefore the kingdom could not have been established before.

The same reading states Bathsheba was David's favorite wife. In the Bible, such passages as 1 Kings 1:11–31 suggest Bathsheba had great influence with the king, and that this was recognized by his counselors. Indeed, she may have been "the woman behind the man" whose love and wisdom may have been an essential source of strength and inspiration for David. She may have had a greater influence on the destiny of the emerging kingdom than is normally supposed and greater importance than just as the mother of Solomon.

Whatever blessing may have flowed from Bathsheba, his alliance with her also occasioned some of David's greatest misfortune and sorrow. "Only in the matter of Uriah the Hittite did David displease God," said Edgar Cayce, "and for that he had to pay heavily." Because of it, the goodness David established did not continue.

Shortly after the adultery with Bathsheba and the death of Uriah, Nathan, the next great prophet after Samuel, was called to pronounce a fearful sentence on David—"The sword shall never depart from your house forever." (2 Samuel 12:10) David reaped a punishing karma from what he had sown—the effects were almost

---

a single sentence without comment or notice taken of it. This attitude toward time remains throughout the whole book.

Even the synoptic gospels cannot be declared chronologically accurate.

The earliest Christian writer to discuss the origin of the gospels, Papias (about 140 A.D.), stated explicitly that Mark wrote "not in order."

instantaneous. The child of their union died. David's daughter Tamar was raped by her brother Amnon, who in turn was murdered by their brother Absalom the beautiful. Absalom then led a rebellion against his father which caused him to flee from Jerusalem. Before Absalom was slain by Joab, he publicly violated all David's wives, which requited what David had done secretly to the wife of Uriah.

From the time of his adultery onward David's otherwise glorious reign was marred with unceasing trouble —all of which had been revealed to Nathan.

An elderly Kansas woman was told in her reading that, preceding an incarnation in Palestine during the time of Jesus, she had been in the court of David as a nurse and instructor to David's children. Nathan's pronouncements had a life-long effect upon this teacher of young Solomon.

... the entity was again in the Holy Land, among the maids or helpers to Bathsheba, the queen of the king David. The entity was active in those periods when there were the questionings and the admonitions delivered to the king by Nathan. These made a great impression upon this entity, then Abjada, making for a keeping closer not only to the tenets but to the spirit of the law through those activities. And as there grew to be those changes wrought by the educating of those that were to rise in power, the entity aided there.

Thus children, children's activities, games, directions, cards, any form of books that may aid children in arousing to an active mind that needed, may be a part of the life experience and the work of the entity in the present.

The entity gained throughout, for it caught the vision and it applied the message in those activities with the training of Solomon through those periods of the early childhood. (3361-1)

As David rose in power, establishing himself over the surrounding nations, many of the kingdoms began to send tribute and gifts to him. The most notable is Hiram, king of Tyre, who furnished cedars, carpenters, and masons as David built his house. This was the beginning of a lasting alliance between the two kingdoms that extended through Solomon's reign.

It is interesting to note that David, whose chief desire was to build the Temple, was allowed only to build his house. Solomon, who was the builder of the Temple, spent less time on it than he did in the construction of his palace.

On May 10, 1944, an owner and manager of a rest home was told she had been a decorator for the homes of these two monarchs.

> . . . the entity was in the land now known as the Holy Land, and among those who were of the children of Judah, during those periods when there were the establishings in the city where the great Temple was built.
>
> The entity was then acquainted with David and Solomon, as a contributor both to the decorations in the Palace of Bathsheba and in the house of the king in Solomon's period.
>
> In the name then Rahalab, the entity gained through those activities because of the counsel, not merely in regard to the preparations in finery.
>
> Thus the entity is at home with the lowly, as well as those in authority or in higher places. Use, don't abuse, those dependencies which arise from the associations in those periods. (5082–1)

The King's Daughter

On August 1, 1934, a stately Jewish woman obtained her Life Reading, and another memorable page in Edgar Cayce's story of the Old Testament was added.

We have an account in the Bible of two children who were born to David and Bathsheba: the child who died as punishment for their adultery, and Solomon, the heir to David's throne.

Yet reading 601–2 describes a third, and most memorable child—the king's daughter.

The first intimation appeared in a reading requesting physical help. Cayce began his diagnosis in the customary manner with an analysis of the blood, and then broke it off immediately to say:

So many things that have rushed in, from the activities or relations of this entity in one experience in its activities in the earth, almost overpower all the rest. She was a daughter, you see, of David. The body should wear the seal of same at all times; the crown or the vase with the crown of the king in same. (601–1)

Cayce then returned to his diagnosis of the body. A question at the conclusion of the reading brought out these additional responses.

Q–8. Is there any other information that may be given this entity that would be of benefit at this time?
A–8. As we have indicated, the seal should be worn at most times about the body; the king's seal. The cup with the king's crown upon same. Either in the form of cameo or other stones. Any stone in which it may be; not as a charm, but rather as that which comes with the lineal activity or descendant, and the influences that come about; for the soul—or entity—was indeed the king's daughter. (601–1)

Three weeks later the first of two life readings concerning this life were given.

. . . we find (wherein much is made manifest in the present sojourn, present activities) the entity was during the reign of that ruler, that king of the Hebrew people who had been called for a purpose in a promised land; and among the daughters of David was the entity numbered; and among the daughters—or *the* daughter of Bathsheba that lived; hence a close relationship, and only mentioned once in the Scriptures— and only in a portion of so much that has been left out.

So, the entity was a sister of Solomon—that also rose to the beauty of the pomp and power. This brought into the experience of the entity all those glories of the two kingdoms; for the entity was among those that were favored, not only of the people but of those that came for counsel—as the people of many nations—to receive, in those associations and relations, words of counsel from the preacher or the teacher in Solomon, and those *greater* in the Psalms of David.

Hence many of these have been to the entity the songs wherein there has come within self much that has lifted up, especially in those instances when it is said, "I was glad when they said unto me, we will go into the house of our God." In this Psalm the entity led often in the meetings of those that counseled for the aid of those that would purify themselves for the services in the various activities. However, as is known, the mothers and daughters were forbidden much of the activities then.

In the name Sheluenmehei, the entity gained much in the experience, and aided the father during those days when Absalom the beautiful rebelled; during those days when darkness came to the peoples through the various changes wrought by the political forces and powers.

Innately from the experience does the entity view and judges well as to political influences, yet keeps aloof in part from interfering or changing much in same. *What* might be given of the experience of the entity during that sojourn!

In the present, though, is seen the very movements or activities, and the associations and relations; the aid and help that the entity not imposes, but graciously offers in its services to others, which has endeared itself to many of those whom the entity has been only as an acquaintance, or more so to those whom the entity has shown itself a friend. For indeed in the carriage and in the naturally innate forces does the entity show itself to be a daughter of the king among kings! (601-2)

The Books of Samuel appear to be almost eye-witness accounts of the reigns of Saul and David. Chronicles contains much material, often word for word, found in other books of the Bible. However in 1 Chronicles, which recounts events in David's reign, everything doubtful and offensive regarding him and his house is omitted. He is presented as being primarily preoccupied with the organization of the Temple services.

The husband of Mrs. 601 obtained a life reading, and Cayce placed him among the sons of Abner, and a suitor in that life to the daughter of Bathsheba.

This reading also indicates that it was not until after the rebellion by Absalom that the accumulation of materials and organization and preparation for the Temple began.

. . . we find the period was when David, the shepherd king, the beloved, ruled the land; and when wars were little, and no more were those activities of . . . Absalom making for the disturbing forces in the experience.

The entity then was among the sons of Abner that made overtures to the daughter of the king, or the daughter of Bathsheba. For the entity then rose to favor with the king, and was active in establishing— with the individuals and peoples nigh unto the land, in Tyre and Sidon—the preparations of the poles of cedar, the posts of cedar, that were to become the timbers in the Temple.

These were the activities of Ajalon, the son of Abner, and the son-in-law of the king.

In the experience the entity was greatly active in bringing about the relationships of those peoples that supplied much for that service in the temple, where the king had purposed in his heart to dedicate a place, a house, to the worship of Jehovah—God.

The entity gained much in the experience, and in the present from same the entity finds that whether the associations are with those within or without the own faith—if they are true to *their* purposes—they are as One! In this has tolerance come, through those experiences and in the application of that in the present—so that this has grown to be a part of the entity's experience. (619–5)

The King's Son-in-Law

In the second life reading for Mrs. 601, we are told Sheluenmehei was betrothed to the prince of Tyre, and that the marriage was the foundation for the lasting alliance between Tyre and Israel. Apparently her present husband (619)—whom Cayce described as the king's son-in-law—married another of his many daughters.

From the historical aspect, the following is one of the most illuminating readings given for this period.

Gertrude Cayce: You will please give in detail the life history of this entity's appearance in the earth as Sheluenmehei, the daughter of David, and the associations of that period . . . You will answer the questions that may be asked concerning that period . . .
Edgar Cayce: Yes, we have the entity, the inquiring mind and the soul-mind of the entity now known as [601]—*now*, and the experience of the soul-entity as Sheluenmehei, the daughter of Bathsheba and David.

In that experience we find, after the death of the child when there was the first coition with Bathsheba, the wife of Uriah, and the king, in the next change was the birth of Sheluenmehei—meaning, a reproach has been removed.

The entity then grew up under the conditions that were the more favorable during those periods of the spreading influence of the king, not only with the peoples but with the nations thereabout.

The mother being the favorite of the king had those advantages that might be accorded one in that position; being an accomplished harpist, or what would be the harp today, and that endeared the entity to the king.

With the changes that came with the rise to power of Joab and his associates Manasseh, Anahasia (?), and Haliel (?), these sought the hand of the king's daughter Sheluenmehei in the connections with the taking of the strongholds of the Philistines; but with the coming of Haran son of Hiram, of Tyre and Sidon, the king's daughter became the bride that cemented the friendships with Hiram who furnished the cedars and the building materials for the king's house.

With the change by that association there was brought the greater development for the entity during the period, and the associations in that period with one in the own household in the present—the present daughter—made for a contribution to the developing conditions for the whole. The relations then were rather the friendships, for the daughter was then that of the Anias(?)—or the brother of Joab's wife's daughter, but not *of* those peoples.

As to the soul development of the entity during the experience: As there has been the close relationships with the king's activities, the law, the psalms, these became a portion of the entity's experience.

Being in an environ that was so changed from that in Jerusalem and that in Tyre, there were brought many longings—and many of those periods when the entity or the soul finds expression in the music. And in the present there are those feelings that when there is that type of music that bespeaks of the *longings* of home, of the temple, of those changes that may come in the experience of a soul, strikes a chord in the entity that may be recognized as an awareness of those longings for the hills, the home in Jerusalem . . .

With the changes that were wrought in the experiences of the entity during the rebellions among the king's sons, when first the conditions arose from Tamar's (a sister, or half-sister) being despoiled by her brother, this made for the change in many of the associations; yet the daughter continued to *visit* with those of the king's household.

With the rebellion of Absalom, this brought turmoil and strife, and the attempt on the part of the daughter to come to the aid of David as he fled from Jerusalem; and with the battle won, the daughter then collapsed (being heavy with child) at the news of the death of Absalom; yet being succored or aided by the king, suffering then in body for a period, and with the birth of Huel, the second son of Haran's that became the king after the death of Hiram, the mother —or the entity—then joined or slept with the fathers; coming, as has been seen, in a later experience in the earth. (601-5)

Absalom's Rebellion

Absalom's rebellion was the most grim and shattering experience in David's life. It was his gravest crisis, and the considerable importance of the rebellion is indicated by the amount of space allotted to it in the Bible, from chapter 13 through 19 in 2 Samuel.

The rebellion divided David's kingdom, caused the defection of some of his advisors, led to the death of his daughter (601), and his son, and, at the end, completely crushed his spirit and broke his heart. And all this had, in some way, been foreseen by Nathan. (2 Samuel 12:10–11) David was a totally different man after Absalom rebelled.

Four life readings refer to Absalom's rebellion in such a way to indicate it was a turning point in David's reign. 601-2 indicates that the spiritual light which was growing in the minds of the people under David's leadership became obscured, and ". . . darkness came . . . through the various changes wrought by the political forces and powers." 619 and 476 show that there was a new thrust of activity when " . . . no more were those activities of . . . Absalom making for the disturbing forces . . ." (619–5) and "As peace began to be restored after the rebellions of Absalom, there came to the entity the greater development . . ." (1073–4)

The rebellion was the final cleansing, or karma from David's adultery with Bathsheba, even to Absalom's fornication with David's wives in broad daylight "in the sight of Israel" to requite what David had done secretly to the wife of Uriah the Hittite. No doubt all the family relationships were charged with karmic overtones, but lack of any additional information precludes any further speculation. However, a definite cycle can be discerned from David's adultery and Nathan's pronouncement to Absalom's death and the paralyzing remorse which gripped David.

When David finally was able to overcome his depression and inaction, he initiated the great period of planning and gathering materials for the Temple which Nathan had revealed would be built by Solomon.

"Here we have all the scandal that could possibly be conceived," Edgar Cayce said as the Bible class began their study of chapter 13 of 2 Samuel. This chapter contains rape and murder and shows the background events which led to the estrangement between father and son which eventually culminated in rebellion.

When Amnon raped Tamar, Absalom avenged his sister by murdering his brother. He then fled to Geshur, the territory where his mother's father was king, and stayed there for three years.

All through this time David wanted to be reconciled with Absalom. Joab, David's general, knew this and also saw a dangerous situation developing with the people who favored Absalom. Perhaps Absalom even then was plotting from afar.

Joab made wise use of the woman of Tekoah who, through her subtle parable, softened David's heart. David ordered Joab to Geshur to bring Absalom home.

Edgar Cayce told his Bible class:

"We can understand how Absalom felt it was up to him to slay Amon, and how David naturally grieved when his oldest son was slain. In those days it was permissible for relatives to marry. No doubt if Amnon had gone about it in the right way, David would have allowed him to have Tamar. However, his whole purpose was evil.

"Joab, the leader of the army, understood Absalom; and he attempted to warn David by sending the wise woman of Tekoah. Notice that she is not referred to as a witch nor as a soothsayer nor as one with a familiar spirit. Whatever else she might have been, she was certainly a good actress. However, David recognized Joab as the source of it. He knew that Joab understood how he wanted to bring back Absalom, and now there was a way it could be done and still save face.

"David punished himself by not allowing himself to see Absalom. This was very unwise. It engendered in Absalom a spirit of rebellion."

We can see how the mistake David made in not seeing his son affected the proud, unrestrained, and "beautiful" Absalom. It must have pricked his ego and goaded his pride to be ignored, and he began plotting the overthrow of his father.

For four years he stood outside the king's gate and offered to take the people's side in any litigation that came before the king. In this way he used political issues to insinuate his way into the hearts of the men of Israel. He plotted, and his conspiracy grew. Soon the majority of the people were on his side.

When Absalom sounded the alarm which signaled the rebellion, his army outnumbered David's, and David was forced to flee Jerusalem.

David, who was much more spiritually conscious than Absalom, refused to fight over an essentially political issue. In a similar vein, it was the same as Jesus refusing to defend himself against his accusers or to resist the way of the cross. David even ordered Zadok and Abia-thar, the two priests who joined him in his retreat, to carry the Ark of God back to the city and to remain with it.

Cayce's remarks stress David's spiritual understanding.

"It became necessary for David to flee Jerusalem. Absalom's army was several times larger than his, and he didn't want Jerusalem destroyed. He had been pre-paring to build the house of the Lord, and he knew why he was not being allowed to build it. From this time on, David attempts to atone for his sin, instead of fighting back. It was not his intention to hurt his son. On every occasion when he might have done harm to Absalom, he wriggled out of it. He ordered the Ark back to the city. He realized the battle was one for material power, and did not pertain to the spiritual life. So he was running away so that the beloved city would be spared, and not destroyed for purely material reasons."

During the flight from Jerusalem, an episode took place which to Edgar Cayce revealed the key to David's true greatness.

During the retreat, at Beth-hurim, Shimei, of the house of Saul, came out and followed David along the side of the road, throwing stones and cursing the king. Shimei shouted angrily that Absalom's revolt was God's way of requiting David for the blood of Saul.

David's soldiers were incensed at this Benjamite's im-pudence and asked permission to cut off his head.

David's reply was characteristic. It indicates more than just his unwillingness to blame others for his troubles. He had not forgotten Nathan's prophecy. He understood this misfortune was in someway connected with his own shortcomings, when he said:

What is it to me and you? Let him curse. It is the Lord who has told him to curse David. Who can say to me, Why has this happened? . . . Let him curse; for God has bidden him. (2 Samuel 16:10–11)

Cayce saw David's character revealed by this response.

"David felt that whatever came, came for a purpose. If we could only learn that lesson today! Misfortune is not for our undoing, but to make us strong. If we can accept it in that light, it becomes a steppingstone and not a stumblingblock in our greater (spiritual) development. If we hold to the good, we can always do something about our problems. *It was because David was able to hold to such an attitude that it can be said of him, 'he was a man after God's heart.'*"

Ahithophel, one of David's most advanced counselors (2 Samuel 16:23) elected to stay with Absalom. Hushai, another trusted advisor, also remained in Jerusalem, but retained his loyalty to David and acted as his agent.

This was Edgar Cayce's lesson.

"Hushai was a very wonderful secret agent for David. Absalom never suspected that Hushai was acting in David's best interests. Being of the nature to seek material position and power, Absalom could understand how Hushai would join with him because he was the stronger. But the fact that Hushai could remain true to David regardless of David's weak position was beyond anything Absalom could understand. This is a good example of how all things work together for good to those who love the Lord.

"David followed Hushai's advice and moved his army across the Jordan, where the people were sympathetic to him. They hadn't fallen under Absalom's spell."

From the other side of the Jordan David mounted his campaign. Once the battle was engaged, David was victorious and Absalom was slain. Although David asked that Absalom be spared, Joab felt the only decisive way to win the battle was to kill him, which he did.

David's deep depression and prolonged sorrow following these events show how deeply he was affected.

David's sons grew up selfish and unrestrained, at least we see this from the examples of Amnon, Absalom, and Adonijah. Indeed if his approach to Adonijah was typical (. . . *at no time did he rebuke him, saying, Why have you done so?* [1 Kings 1:6]), David must have been the prototype of the ultra-permissive parent.

With the rebellion over, David went through a period of deep soul-searching and introspection as he reviewed the wreckage in his household and his kingdom.

Edgar Cayce felt David's extreme reaction was from a sense of personal guilt.

"David continued to be sorrowful over Absalom's death. This was unusual. When his and Bathsheba's first child died, he ceased to mourn when there was no longer anything he could do. Perhaps he had a guilty conscience, and felt he could have prevented things from turning out as they had. He was beginning to realize he had failed to raise his children properly. If he had, this kind of thing could not have happened. He felt the whole thing was an outgrowth of some failure on his part.

"David was indulging in self-pity. Joab brought him back to his senses. He made David realize he was responsible for the future welfare of the kingdom. The whole nation looked to him for guidance."

With David's return to Jerusalem, he began the great work of planning and preparing for the construction of the Temple, which was not to be built in his life-time. Like Moses, David advanced the great purpose and cause of Israel, but did not live to enjoy the fruits of his greatest labor.

The great work helped take David's mind off the past. By putting his energies into the organization of the Temple, David brought healing to himself, his house, and his nation.

In this reading, a Jewish opera singer was told she was a grandchild of David's, the daughter of Adonijah, the son who rebelled when David was near his deathbed:

... we find the entity was in the land now known as the Holy Land, during those periods when the shepherd king was in order—or ruled.

It was during those periods when turmoil and strife arose through the rebellions within the household of the king—or David.

The entity then was among the daughters of Adonijah, who was among the first of the sons of David.

As peace began to be restored after the rebellions of Absalom, there came to the entity the greater development as it joined with the sons and daughters and the folk of the king to make preparations for the establishing and the building of the house of the Lord.

Hence we find within the entity's innate experience a reverence for those things that have been blessed even by man, or that have been dedicated ... to that he worships as the spirit of truth and hope in his relationships to Creative Forces.

Songs create a reverence, or those things of the nature that tend to make for a reverential inspiration —or blessings, or prayer.

The entity was among the first to set the Twenty-fourth Psalm to music, or that which is now called a portion of the Twenty-fourth Psalm. For the entity enjoyed the music of the grandfather upon the harp.

In the name then of Besne-berea, it may be said that the entity gained; especially in the latter part of its sojourn ... (1073–4)

Footnotes to an Era

It is said that the most perfectly written lines in the English language are, "O my son Absalom, my son, my son Absalom! would God I had died for thee, O Absalom, my son, my son!" (2 Samuel 18:33) They ring with the same compassion, sadness, and love as Jesus' words, "O Jerusalem, Jerusalem." (Matthew 23:37; Luke 13:34)

For Mrs. 601, Cayce used the verse as a lesson on love.

Q-. How can I help those nearest and dearest to higher development?

A-1. In pointing those principles as held innately and manifestedly in self, that what ye do unto thy fellow man is that by which ye will be judged before the Throne. For when an unkind thought, an unkind deed is done within the *mind*—or the soul-mind of an entity —it builds that which makes for the interference with the will and desire of the spirit association within self; or the conscience will smite thee.

Then, in aiding others; just being kind, showing forth that love as the entity heard: "O Absalom, Absalom, my son Absalom! would God I had died for thee!" This will bring, as the entity says same to self, a change in the feelings as respecting what love—LOVE— means. (601-5)

Another description in Mrs. 601's reading supplies an additional important footnote to this era—the king's seal!

The King's Seal

Edgar Cayce described a gift from King David to his daughter in Tyre.

The seal that the entity wore then, as the gift from the king, should ever be about the body. This we would give in some detail:

A cross; each prong being the same length, you see. Cut as a shadow box in its making. On the cross, the rosette of the king. In the center of the rosette a raised figure; or *plane*, and *on* this plane *this* figure: Draw a seven. Draw it! In the front *raise* the upper line of the seven, see? In front of this line draw a mark slanting towards the right; *heavy*, and slanting almost straight down. On the back side of the seven a line leaning towards the seven, you see, just a little space from same. This, of course, represents the Hebraic characters of the cabalistic intent or import; meaning El Yah(?)—God Preserves! (601-5)

In connection with the seal, Cayce made a prophecy.

Q-4. If possible, please give information as to where I can find a design of King David's seal, which it was suggested that I should wear?
A-4. Make as has been indicated. It will *one* day be uncovered in Jerusalem.
Q-5. Of what would it be best for it to be made?
A-5. Either ivory, coral, or gold; or ivory inlaid with gold; or gold with the raised figure of the rosette and the letter.
Q-6. Is there any further advice that would be helpful to me at this time?
A-6. Much may be given. These we would think and ponder over. Keep these close in the heart. (601-5)

A Brother to Solomon

A reading for a young Alabama man adds another portrait to the gallery of David's sons. Apparently this one, like the others, was a disappointment.

The reading began in an interesting manner, pointing to a lesson.

For what a body-mind, a soul-mind does about or with the knowledge or understanding that it has makes for development for that soul. For some beautiful comparisons may be drawn from the entity's own experiences in the earth. For, while the entity was an associate or a brother to Solomon in an experience, what one did with his knowledge and understanding and what the other did with his understanding made for quite a difference in each one's position in that experience and the [following] sojourns of each soul in other experiences. (476-1)

The reading indicates David was unable to impress his own spiritual understanding upon this son who, under the reign of Solomon, became a tax gatherer or assessor in his commercial enterprises.

. . . we find the entity was in that period when David was ruler in the promised land, and among David's sons we find the entity's activities—Ajalon. These we find in a contention again, though reasonable to many; yet to self the activities brought not the use of the knowledge obtained through the counsel of the father (earthly) as to become wholly acceptable—either in the spiritual or the material things in the experience. There were contentions with Absalom, who won the hearts of the people, and associations with the sister of Absalom in an unethical manner. The associations with that son who became the ruler, and known as the "wise one," brought rather both mental and physical development to the entity, yet in the spiritual or soul forces rather a standstill—or non-development, as seen in the next experience . . . * In the application of self in the present experience, however, that sojourn may be said to be that one which may influence the entity in the present to a greater degree. For, the activities may be turned into fields—not of a political nature, neither wholly commercial, yet that deal with both—where gatherings of sales or taxes may be in the experience of the entity, from the purely material sense, the activities in which the greater strides or successes may be made. As to what the entity may do respecting its soul or spiritual development depends upon the application of the knowledge and understanding, and as to whether or not the trust and the ideal is put in these influences that may guide, guard and keep the soul in the way of the Lamb.

Hence as an assessor, a tax gatherer, a statistician, in such fields of activity, the entity may find the greater successes in the present . . . for the entity's *material* development. (476–1)

*About the time of William the Conqueror and the Norman Invasion, the entity incarnated "with a grudge" which made him "a natural leader," but for destructive rather than constructive purposes.

Chapter 8

The Golden Age of Solomon

Under Solomon Israel reached the apex of its glory. The Spirit manifested more fully in the affairs of men than it had ever done before. Wealth, Culture, Power, and Worship all flowered in an Age of Peace. Yet a few short years after his death, Solomon's Temple and Palace were sacked, the first of many times. Its brief existence has raised the notion that the real purpose for the glories of Solomon was to hold up an assurance, a preview of the glories of the millennial reign of Christ.

We know that the reign of Christ has always existed, but begins individually, with the discovery of the Christ within. It is a spiritual law, however, that before entering into any new dimension of spiritual understanding, we will be tried and tested in our faith. Before entering the promised land, the children of Israel were tested in the wilderness. On the threshold of the Golden Age, the people were tested under Saul. As in the wilderness, they were confronted with a mass of conflicting forces and urges and given the opportunity to choose whom they would serve. Saul and David are like the brothers Cain and Abel, or Jacob and Esau—representing the two principles of worldliness and self-gratification as opposed to selflessness through service and the seeking of Truth.

Those like Jonathan, who grew to understand why Saul was rejected, learned why David was accepted.

God chose David because David chose Him. Saul could not overcome his own self-interests, while David tried to keep God's Will first and foremost. By choosing David the people were choosing God. When a sufficient number followed the young king, they were cooperating with God's Plan of redemption by becoming "a helpmeet with Him in bringing that to pass that all may be one with Him." (281–16) Those who lived with David and were loyal to his purposes laid the foundation for the Golden Age, the greatest epoch in Israel's unfoldment since the time of Joshua.

The Kingdom Within

As a symbol for possibilities and potential in man's experience, the Golden Age of Solomon is equally as vital and inclusive a symbol as the Garden of Eden or the Promised Land. It exists outside time and space as something which can be looked back upon in history as an assurance, and forward to as an experience. From the Cayce readings we have the understanding that, like all other symbols in the Bible, this unprecedented "Golden Age" can be related a state of mental and physical development with a spiritual equivalent which can be experienced on the inner-planes of consciousness.

Solomon made two enduring contributions to Israel: its wisdom literature and its Temple. Yet Solomon only completed that which David had begun. By building the Temple, Solomon was putting into material form the spiritual perceptions of David.

When David turned over the plans and patterns for the Temple to Solomon, he acknowledged that the Spirit had guided him in all the work. (1 Chronicles 28:19) God himself designed the Temple. Like the Ark of the Covenant and the Tabernacle, the Temple conformed to a pre-existent spiritual pattern which had been received through revelation and inspiration.

David's willingness to be led by the Spirit guided him to the highest possible conceptions about architecture, music, and ritual worship. All was according to God's purpose and his plan of Redemption. This brought into manifestation a material image through which man could eventually come to understand himself. For the Temple represents the Body, the glorified body of Man. There is a pattern within Man which Man may awaken to and experience—the Temple of the Living God where nothing within is less valuable than silver and gold.

Draw from those activities the fact that the body-physical is indeed the Temple of the living God, just as much as the Temple in which there were the material sacrifices offered. So there may be mental and material sacrifices offered and experienced in the present, if the needs would be met for the building of the determination to fill the purpose for which each soul enters a material experience. (2054-2)
... the understanding that there must be—and would be, through the very expression of that Being in the earth—the understanding that the law was written in the hearts of men, rather than upon tablets of stone; that the Temple, that the holy of holies was to be within. (587-6)

The Temple became the focus in this reading:

Thy body is indeed the Temple of the living God. Hold to that. By might and main of the mind, attempt to make the best, the most beautiful, the most acceptable Temple according to thy concept of a living Christ Consciousness. Hold to that. Let no one, in any manner, take that from you.
Then apply, in an expectant manner, those measures which will aid the body-forces to create within self those influences necessary for this building of the body to a beautiful Temple to thy God. (2968-1)
... ye that have seen the light know in Whom thou hast believed, and know that in thine own body, thine own mind, there is set the Temple of the living God, and that it may function in thy dealings with thy fellow man in such measures that ye become as rivers

of light, as fountains of knowledge, as mountains of strength, as the pastures for the hungry, as the rest for the weary, as the strength for the weak. (281–28)

Nothing in Solomon's Temple was less valuable than silver and gold. What a suggestion this is as to our true worth when we become Temples of the Living Spirit.

And, as the entity has learned in the present, the body is indeed the Temple, and that the pattern given in the mount is that pattern of the individual entity or self as it is set up and hedged about, and yet is the place where man meets his Maker. (3129–1)
. . . the body is indeed the Temple of the living God and must be considered and treated as such . . . a channel through which greater help, greater means of expression of self in the present may be brought into being.
For it is THERE—in thine own Temple—as He gave—that He has promised to meet thee! (1598–1)

Portrait of a King

Solomon's reign begins with a vision and a promise.

Then the Lord appeared to Solomon in a vision by night; and God said to him, Ask that which I should give you.
And Solomon said . . . O Lord God, thou hast made thy servant king in the place of David my father; and I am but a little child; I know not how to go out or come in among thy people, whom thou hast chosen . . . Give therefore to thy servant an understanding heart to judge thy people and to discern between good and bad; for who is able to judge this thy so great a people?
And it pleased the Lord because Solomon had asked this thing. And the Lord said to Solomon, Because you have asked this thing and have not asked for yourself riches, neither have you asked the lives of your ene-

mies nor have you asked for yourself long life, but have asked for yourself wisdom to discern judgment; Behold, I have done according to your words; lo, I have given you a wise and understanding heart, so that there has been none like you before you, neither shall any arise after you like you.

And I have given you that which you have not asked, both riches and honor, so that there shall not be any among the kings like you all your days.

And if you will walk in my ways, to keep my statutes and my commandments, as your father David did walk, then I will lengthen your days.

And Solomon awoke; and, behold, it was a dream. (1 Kings 3:5–15; see also 2 Chronicles 1:7–12)

"No fairer promise of true greatness, or more beautiful picture of youthful piety is known in history." Modern critics dismiss this story as a romantic myth. Yet in Edgar Cayce's own life he had a youthful experience which bears marked similarities to young Solomon's. The incident was one of Edgar Cayce's most cherished memories, and is related in full in *There Is a River*, the biography of Edgar Cayce by Tom Sugrue, and retold for children in *The Vision and the Promise*, by Vada Carlson.

Edgar Cayce became an avid reader of the Bible in his early teens, spending hours alone with it, totally immersed in its contents. One day while reading the book outdoors in a special lean-to he had constructed in the woods behind the family house, he became aware of a strange presence. He looked up and saw a woman standing before him. The sun was bright and his eyes could not focus quickly after staring at the pages for so long. He thought his mother had come to bring him home for chores.

The woman spoke, and the young Cayce knew the voice did not belong to his mother, or anyone else he knew. It was like music, he said, soft-spoken and very clear.

"Your prayers have been heard," she said, and then posed the same question as was asked of Solomon: "Tell me what you would like most of all, so that I may give it to you."

He had just finished reading about the vision of Manoah from the Book of Judges. He saw the outline of wings in the woman's shadow. He was frightened. This was an angel! He tried to speak, but no words came out. Scenes of Jesus and his disciples flashed across his mind. Then another shock! He heard himself talking.

"Most of all," he stammered, "I would like to be helpful to others, and especially to children when they are sick."

Suddenly the woman was gone. She was no longer there. He looked at the spot where she had stood, trying to see her in the beams of light, but he was all alone.

Not long after this experience, the vision was confirmed. Cayce discovered he had the ability to put himself to sleep, and while in this self-induced trance state, able to diagnose physical illness. Shortly after this discovery, he was asked to help a five-year-old girl, Aime Dietrich, who had been seriously ill for three years. Her parents had been told she could never be healed. In trance, Cayce described the source of her illness and prescribed treatments. The parents followed the recommendations and the child recovered her health.

This was the first of thousands that confirmed the young boy's vision and the promise it contained.

This experience was one among many which demonstrated through his own life the hypothesis he advanced as a student and teacher of the Bible—that everything recorded in Scripture is capable of being experienced. Or, as said in one reading:

Condemn no one. Love all. Do good. And ye may experience it all. (281–30)

Cayce accepted Solomon's experience as authentic. He could relate it to his own, and thus was spared the necessity of seeking elaborate explanations or rationalizations.

When it came time to discuss Solomon's vision in the Bible class, Cayce drew upon views created by reflections on his youth.

"Solomon expressed humbleness. He realized he was completely new at the business of receiving guidance from God. Also, his had been a rather sheltered life. He had been protected and had not accomplished great things like his father had done when still a young man.

"None before Solomon requested such a thing, and none after him has been given the same unique opportunity as he had. Solomon was given a choice, just as everyone is. How we use that choice is completely an individual matter."

Although Cayce apparently was born with a love for God and a desire to serve, he never consciously set out to be a psychic. It wasn't until he reached middle-age that he made psychic diagnosing a full-time and lifelong work. From the age of thirteen, he had been guided, led and shown—often unwillingly—how that youthful vision would be fulfilled.

That acquired wisdom is reflected in his next comment.

"If the Lord appeared to us today, would we understand our place among our friends, our neighbors sufficiently, to know what ability we had which could best serve them? If not, whose fault would it be? Not the Lord's, but ours. God always knows what's best—but it is necessary for us to know also the best manner in which we may serve.

"Solomon made a wise choice. We also could make that choice, by asking not for ourselves, for long life or riches, but that we might have judgment to deal with the problems with which we are faced."

Another Dream

Two years after Edgar Cayce made his decision to engage full-time in psychic work, he dreamed he talked to King Solomon. An interesting tradition in Jewish lore is that anyone who dreams of Solomon will be given wisdom.

The dream occurred in December, 1925, shortly after Cayce completed the decisive move to Virginia Beach, Virginia, the location his own readings had stated would be the most conducive for his work. The interpretation reveals how deeply Cayce searched for wisdom, and also contained a warning.

Q–6. Tuesday night, December 15, or Wednesday morning, December 16. Dreamed of talking with King Solomon.
A–6. In this we find the entity in that manner and way in which the inmost forces of self seek the wisdom that is given to him of whom it has been said, "None shall rise that in physical will be mightier in wisdom than he."

In this seeking, then, we find that attunement that should be used by [the] entity in seeking out those ways to carry on the work as has been set before same; being wise in every way, without the weaknesses of the flesh as were in that entity, see? (294–53)

Pages of Wisdom

Three thousand proverbs and 1,005 songs are attributed to Solomon. (1 Kings 4:32) His wisdom ranged from the mysteries of life to everything known about the animal, vegetable, and mineral kingdoms. So schooled was Solomon about the natural world, legend states he was able to communicate with animals. When judging a case, he knew instinctively which party was guilty and did not need the presence of witnesses.

Is such a life unobtainable in the present day? Even the legendary Renaissance men could not match the accomplishments of this genius. But we may find parallels in Cayce's life to match Solomon.

His 14,246 psychic readings preserved and on file in Virginia Beach attest to his ability to tune in to an Infinite source of knowledge and wisdom. The subject matter in these discourses comprises thousands of topics and touches upon all aspects of Man—his spirit, his soul, his God, his mind, and his body. Just as Solomon's reputation in his day drew earnest seekers from all walks of life to query the king, the unerring accuracy of the Cayce readings draws researchers and seekers from all parts of the world to Virginia Beach. Thousands of individuals from all walks of life have found in the Cayce material practical and applicable as well as astounding truths which have enhanced the quality of their lives.

Cayce's sensitivities are also part of the lore that surrounds his life. His abilities to see and read auras made him an unnerving judge of character. He was a conscious telepathist and clairvoyant. Although there are no stories about him talking to animals, his ability to see and communicate with departed entities is well-known.

However, with all his accomplishments and gifts, the impression one receives from Edgar Cayce is not of a great intellect or gifted genius. His conscious wisdom is shown through spiritual sensitivity applied to practical matters. He cloaked himself in an aura of humility, and all his life strove to be "a common man."

While Cayce may not be a particularly good example of a genius, Solomon is not an archetype of spirituality.

Solomon towers over his reign and projects himself as its most important figure. With so much genius attached to his name, one may feel awed by the shadow he casts and diminished by our own feeble ability to match any of his accomplishments. Edgar Cayce will never be considered the most important aspect of his own legacy, for he completely subordinated himself to the Source which flowed through him. His work in no way diminishes a man, for it continually holds up the promise, "Greater things than these you can do if the Spirit is allowed to work through you."

Solomon Goes Astray

Solomon's vision contained a promise of wealth which, when it came true, must have exceeded the dimensions Solomon himself might have imagined. Solomon's wisdom made him one of the richest men in history; while Cayce's enabled him to live a sparse life with the consolation of faith that his daily needs would be met.

Yet Edgar Cayce knew the temptation that prosperity brings. The wisdom came again from personal experience.

"How was it that Solomon went astray, having been given an understanding heart and deserving such a gift? Perhaps it was the same old story, 'The woman Thou gavest me—SHE persuaded me.'

"Very few people can stand prosperity and Solomon was not one of the few. We can understand from his life what Jesus meant when he said it is easier for the camel to pass through the eye of the needle than for a rich man to enter the kingdom.

"In the beginning of Solomon's reign, he approached God always with the statement, 'I remember what you did for my father David.' But after many years of worldly things, his heart was drawn away from God. Too many riches, too much wine and women made it harder and harder for Solomon to hold to his ideal."

In the worldly sense, Edgar Cayce never knew financial security. Although this lack occasionally disturbed him, it was a greater concern to his friends and associates than it was to himself. One reading indicated that at one level of the mind, Edgar Cayce was withholding the flow of abundance from him. The financial stress resulted from "an innate fear in self" regarding his ability to withstand the temptations prosperity would bring. A life reading also indicated the condition was karmic, stemming from a past life in which Cayce had misused his psychic abilities for material gain.

Edgar Cayce realized in his latter years that had he been financially successful in his youth, he might possibly have abandoned spiritual work altogether, and certainly would not have obtained the purity of purpose and ideal his poverty imposed upon him.

Ultimately Solomon lost his hold not only on his own faith but on his people as well.

Although Cayce in his lifetime never really knew wealth, power, or reknown, except in a very limited way, the indication is that he was faithful to the end, and thus earned his crown, a crown of lasting life. (James 1:12, Revelation 2:10)

The Courts of Solomon: They Were There

Asaph
. . . The king's seer in the matters of God
(Chronicles 25:5)

It would be peculiar indeed if the soul who, as one reading states, (5322–1) supplied the purpose for the whole Bible to be written; who caused the line of Israel to come into existence; who had been Adam, Enoch, Melchizedek, Joseph, and Joshua, was not reincarnated during the Golden Age of Jewish history. It does not seem likely that this soul who had experienced every phase of the national development would by-pass the opportunity to experience its highest achievement and further its glory.

Yet the Edgar Cayce readings say little and offer scant clues. When asked about the important incarnations in the development of Jesus, we find no reference to this period.

Q–19. Please list the names of the incarnations of the Christ, and of Jesus, indicating where the development of the man Jesus began.
A–19. First, in the beginning, of course; and then as Enoch, Melchizedek, in the perfection. Then in the earth, of Joseph, Joshua, Jeshua, Jesus. (5749–14)

But when asked which incarnations of Adam were the most significant in terms of the world's development, we find a slightly amended list, with the name of Asaph appearing on it.

Q-6. Please give the important reincarnations of Adam in the world's history.
A-6. In the beginning as Amilius, as Adam, as Melchizedek, as Zend, as Ur,° as *Asaph,* as Jeshua, Joseph, Jesus. (364-7)

The second, and only other direct reference by name to Asaph, is found in reading 364-8, as Cayce again enumerates the incarnations of Jesus.

... as in the periods ... when He walked with men as the Master among men, or when as Joseph in the kingdoms that were raised as the saving of his peoples that *sold* him into bondage, or as in the priest of Salem ... Or, as in those days as Asapha or Affa, [or] in those periods when those of that same Egyptian land were giving those counsels to the many nations [as Hermes or Enoch] ... (364-8)

Another intimation is found in a life reading for a person who had incarnated during the time of Joshua and Moses and the period of David and Solomon.

Hold fast to that thou didst give to thine peoples when thy self, thine inner self, supplied strength not only to the leaders of men—as Moses and Aaron and Joshua —but to that which *became* the strength of the musi-

Q-2. In the Persian experience as San (or Zend) did Jesus give the basic teachings of what became Zoroastrianism?
A-2. In all those periods that the basic principle was the Oneness of the Father, He has walked with men. (364-8)
Q-1. In what country, and in connection with what religion or philosophy, did Jesus live as Ur?
A-1. Ur was rather a land, a place, a city—and the thought, or intent, or the call was from Ur. Ur, then, as presented or represented in the experience of Jesus, as one that impelled or guided those thoughts in that period, or experience. (364-9)

cian [Asaph,] and of him [David] of whom it was said, "the Lord loved him." (1035–1)

Although these are only scant references and no secondary details are given, it is generally assumed by students of the readings that the Asaph (or Affa) mentioned in the incarnations of Jesus refers to Asaph the choirmaster.

Asaph was the founder and eponym of a musical guild within the priestly tribe of the Levites. Twelve psalms are attributed to Asaph. Thus he has a distinct place among those who are believed to have composed and developed the present collection of Psalms, a list which includes Adam, Melchizedek, Abraham, and Moses.

Under his direction, the "sons of Asaph" prophesied with lyres, harps, and cymbals. (1 Chronicles 25:1) Some traditions give Asaph the title attributed to Heman (25:5), "the king's seer in the matters of God."

It is not difficult to ascertain why Asaph was included among the most significant incarnations of Adam in terms of the world's development. Music is a universal language. Music alone can span the space from the spiritual realms to the spheres of material activity. (3509–1)

The entity's music may be the means of arousing and awakening the best of hope, the best of desire, the best in the heart and soul of those who will and do listen. Is not music the universal language, both for those who would give praise and those who are sorry in their hearts and souls? Is it not a means, a manner of universal expression? Thus, may the greater hope come. (2156–1)

One of the most widely recognized effects of music is its ability to change moods. Despair, depression, and hopelessness can be lifted through music into faith, hope, and inspiration. Music can also reach into the deeper areas of the soul and awaken intuitive knowledge of who we are, where we came from, where we are going.

Descriptions in the life readings for this period indicate many came from all parts of the world to hear the inspired interpretations of the psalms, songs, and poems of David and Solomon. Stimulated and imbued with new consciousness and understanding, presumably these visitors returned to their native lands and shared the message with their neighbors.

Thus Asaph's influence upon world religion began in his own lifetime and has continued to the present. Today, the only part of the Old Testament familiar to many Christians is the Psalms. This is also true in other world religions.

As valuable as music is in changing moods and altering consciousness, the description of the Temple dedication indicates Asaph may have known another use and schooled his musicians in the art of raising vibrations for an epiphany.

And it came to pass, when the priests were come out of the holy place (for all the priests who were present there entered into the holy place; also the Levites, who were the singers, all of them of Asaph, of Heman, of Jeduthun, with their sons and their brethren, being arrayed in white linen, having cymbals and psalteries and harps, stood at the east end of the altar, and with them an hundred and twenty priests sounding with trumpets);

That the trumpeters and singers were as one, to make one sound to be heard in praising and thanking the Lord; and they that lifted up their voices with the trumpets and cymbals and instruments of music, and praised the Lord, saying, For he is good; for his mercy endures forever; that then the house was filled with a cloud, even the house of the Lord, so that the priests could not stand to minister because of the cloud; for the house of the Lord was filled with the brightness of his glory. (2 Chronicles 5:11–14)

The undisputed genius of Solomon was in the field of trade and commerce. He recognized the commercial possibilities in Arabia before anyone else, and knew fantastic riches would follow the man who could organize the trade of the early world.

The Phoenicians were the great sailors of this period. The pact between David and Hiram of Tyre continued into the reign of Solomon. This alliance enabled Israel to profit from Phoenician shipbuilding and navigational personnel and experience.

Hiram and Solomon sent out regularly scheduled trade missions that took up to three years to accomplish. Cyrus Gordon in his book *Before Columbus* asserts that the quest for metals, stones, and valued materials such as ivory and special woods impelled the great merchant kings to launch expeditions to the ends of the earth. Gordon states that the Semitic IBRZL meaning "land of iron" most likely is Brazil.

In his book, Dr. Gordon puts forth an impressive array of archeological, linguistic, and cultural evidence which points to the existence of an extensive prehistoric maritime trading empire in which the cultures of Asia, Europe, and America enjoyed widespread contact with each other. Thus the Phoenicians no doubt inherited a legacy from the Minoans who in turn had benefitted from the advancements of an earlier civilization. Dr. Charles Hapgood in his *Maps of the Ancient Sea Kings* also sees evidence in his studies of ancient maps of a superior prehistoric maritime empire whose maps were copied and recopied and in use through the time of Columbus.

Edgar Cayce's description's of Atlantis include expeditions which were sent to all parts of the world, to points as widely separated as Mexico and China, in vehicles which included airships and submarines.

Dr. Hapgood and Dr. Gordon indicate the technology of this empire was not completely lost, but preserved and passed down in one form or another from a period of at least 6000 B.C. The Cayce information suggests an even older period and a more advanced civilization than the two scientists are willing to acknowledge. The *Critias* of Plato suggests the priests of Egypt preserved the knowledge of Atlantis which was transmitted through the priests and initiates of the ancient religions.

No doubt the knowledge of sea routes and lost continents were preserved with the esoteric lore. This information must have been communicated to Solomon. Indeed, the readings would suggest the Israelites had access to all the knowledge of the world.

The Minoan, Phoenician, and Greek empires all maintained a policy of establishing colonies to look after the commercial interests of the homeland. Solomon settled Israelites at key points beyond Israel's borders. We may assume, with Dr. Gordon, that Solomon followed this same policy in all parts of the world. Later these colonies may have played an important role in offering places of refuge for the "lost" tribes during the invasions from Assyria and Babylon.

Although Israel, in the main, is a land-loving people, three tribes are described as navigational: Dan, Zebulon, and Asher. (Genesis 49:13 and Judges 5:17) They must have played an important part in the organization of Solomon's trading fleet. The fleet was manned chiefly by Phoenicians, but comprised other nationalities as well. Greeks were a great seafaring people and some researchers, like Cyrus Gordon and Manly Hall, see in their myths about voyages to unknown lands to the West evidence of contact with the American continent.

The following describes a Greek who joined Solomon's fleet and later rose to a favored position in the court.

On November 27, 1942, a New York City book publisher was told:

> . . . the entity was in the Grecian land, when there were those rumors of those activities in the Holy Land, as called; when the son of David was made king; when those ships of Hiram, the ships of the new king began to ply the waters about the land.

The entity then joined in those activities, that there might be the adventure of seeing, of knowing, of experiencing the stories or tales that had become as hearsay to that awakening people.

The entity became as one favored, eventually, in the court of Solomon, and thus first understood those deeper intents and purposes that must prompt individual activities in material adventures in relationship with things, conditions, experiences.

Then the entity was gifted in making those pronouncements, those announcements of the king during portions of Solomon's reign.

The name then was Persus. In that experience we find there was the development of those things that are innately a part of the present consciousness of the entity; character, strength of body, of mind, the interest the entity experiences in all those influences that develop body; athletics, food values for body building, those things for mind building. All of these are a part of the consciousness from that experience. (2834-1)

The Wise One

This age of wisdom covered all realms of knowledge, both esoteric and exoteric. Few times has so much light shown through so many in such a small area. Solomon's legendary genius derives in a large measure from the creative court which surrounded him. Genius, spirit, and talent clustered around the king. The mark of a great leader is determined by his counselors.

In this reading an actress was told she had been a friend of Solomon's. As a wise counselor in his court, her intuitive knowledge added to Solomon's renown.

Before that the entity was in the "city beautiful" during those activities and periods of the wealth of the world, the renown of that phase of ability, that were a part of the experience of that era; during the reign of King Solomon.

The entity then was a close companion of, and an interpreter for the king. For, through the activities in which there was the interpreting of the law, the interpreting of poetry and songs of the period, the entity induced the friendships in many of the other lands.

Then the entity was in the name Jethebeth, AND a companion of that king. From same in the present we find there are those experiences and feelings that may be as dreams, or those visions that have been a part of the experience, in the formulas that have been the attempt of the entity at times, to turn to the innate self.

In the true way may the entity find much, for the entity answered for the king even to that princess that came to question Solomon during that period. (2598–2)

Two Apshas

As did knowledge and commercial wealth, music and ritual worship also reached their culmination in this period.

Three musicians of this period appear in the life readings. Two of the three were given the same name—Apsha.

Apsha was the eponym of the musical guild within the Levites. His name and its variants may have been common, perhaps indicating title or rank.

Solomon's majestic Temple crowded out all the other cults and shrines in Israel. The lofty services and imageless worship of an Unseen God were an effective stimulus upon the inmost reaches of man, counterbalancing the immediate appeal to the sensually gratifying pagan cults. Trained musicians were skilled in the use of music to lift man's consciousness.

A young and gifted musician obtained life reading 5056. He was told in pre-Adamic Atlantis he had been "a real musician on the pipes and reeds," and in the following incarnation, during the days of Solomon, was trained for Temple service. However, Solomon had a different use for his skills.

Before that we find the entity was in the activities in the Temple of Solomon in Jerusalem when there was the choosing by David of those who were to be prepared for the service of music in the Temple which was yet to be built. David chose young men and they were given the physical as well as the mental and spiritual training through the activities in the preparations in the school as had been undertaken or begun by Elijah in Carmel.

Thus the entity in the name Apsha was among those who were in the Temple service when the activities were begun through those periods of Solomon's reign. Those were the periods when there was the great amount of what today would be called notoriety, or during those periods when the Queen of Sheba visited Solomon, the entity was chosen as the one to make music for Solomon to make love by, to the Queen. (5056–1)

In his next life, the entity studied music under St. Cecilia, the patron saint of musicians. Music became a source of sexual stimulation for 5056, and he became enamored of the saint and desired her physically. Music was forgotten, and, being rebuffed, he eventually destroyed himself.

The second Apsha is found in a life reading given for an eleven-month-old child on September 8, 1941. The entity is described as among the chief musicians in the Temple. This Apsha held to the purpose of using music to attune the mind for worship. The influence of this life carried over into his next—as Franz Liszt. The great Hungarian pianist and composer again was a leader in expressing the spiritual qualities of music.

Before that the entity was in the earth during those periods of the preparation and the accomplishing of the setting up of the music in the Temple that was planned by David and completed by Solomon.

The entity was an associate then of both David and Solomon, being among the chief musicians for setting the psalms to the order of preparation for the various instruments upon which there would be the music for services in the temples. And the psalms of David as well as the songs of Solomon were a part of the entity's experience, in their preparation, as well as the psalms and the musical activities in which the entity engaged.

Then the entity was in the name Apsha. In the experience the entity gained. For there were those attempts ever to keep the activities in the service such that they appealed to the minds of those who would come to worship. Also there were the constant attempts to attain or gain favor with those in authority, and to impress upon them—in the various ways and manners—the needs of their being leaders, as individuals, in the spiritual and mental attributes as well as the material.

Here, too, will be the needs for the instructions to the entity through the formative years, by those upon whom the entity is dependent for an environment in which there may be kept the spiritual, the mental, and the material experiences well balanced in the activities throughout the developing years. (2584-1)

The Dreamer

Perhaps the only appropriate note to end upon is with a dreamer and her memories. *Mind is the Builder,* as the Cayce readings so often remind us; and without dreaming, the mystery and splendor of the higher truths could never enter into the mind of man.

Divisions, boundaries, limitations blur and alter as we awaken to the Divine Within. The Seen and Unseen are unable to be separated. The point of demarcation between imagination and fact cannot be found. As Consciousness becomes spiritualized, all becomes One.

The third musician in the readings was a court entertainer. A middle-aged New Hampshire widow was told:

. . . the entity was in the holy city, or Jerusalem, during those periods when there was a great splendor indicated in the activities; during the reign of Solomon.

The entity was among the entertainers—a musician —in the royal palace.

The love of indolence, the love of quiet, the abilities as the musician as well as the love of the mystery and the splendor that goes with the dreaming of same, are all a part of the experience. The entity gained, the entity lost, the entity gained throughout that period of activity.

Then the name was Rhouel (2576–1)

"It has not yet entered into the mind of man those glories which God has prepared for those who love his ways." The purpose of the Bible is to put into man's mind an understanding of God's Love and man's relationship to it. The Cayce readings are rich with vital, living concepts about the variety and depth of man's inner nature and his spiritual potential. We begin to see what the Throne of David and the Halls of Solomon tell us about our own souls.

Indeed, the Cayce readings, correlated with the Bible, do allow man "to dream."

Index

203

204